LAYERS OF LEARNING

YEAR FOUR • UNIT EIGHT

WORLD WAR I
PLAINS STATES
EARTHQUAKES
EXPRESSIONISM

Published by HooDoo Publishing
United States of America
© 2017 Layers of Learning
Copies of maps or activities may be made for a particular family or classroom. All other rights reserved. Printed in the United States of America.
(Grilled Cheese BTN Font) © Fonttdiner - www.fontdiner.com
ISBN #978-1546744788

Units at a Glance: Topics For All Four Years of the Layers of Learning Program

1	History	Geography	Science	The Arts
1	Mesopotamia	Maps & Globes	Planets	Cave Paintings
2	Egypt	Map Keys	Stars	Egyptian Art
3	Europe	Global Grids	Earth & Moon	Crafts
4	Ancient Greece	Wonders	Satellites	Greek Art
5	Babylon	Mapping People	Humans in Space	Poetry
6	The Levant	Physical Earth	Laws of Motion	List Poems
7	Phoenicians	Oceans	Motion	Moral Stories
8	Assyrians	Deserts	Fluids	Rhythm
9	Persians	Arctic	Waves	Melody
10	Ancient China	Forests	Machines	Chinese Art
11	Early Japan	Mountains	States of Matter	Line & Shape
12	Arabia	Rivers & Lakes	Atoms	Color & Value
13	Ancient India	Grasslands	Elements	Texture & Form
14	Ancient Africa	Africa	Bonding	African Tales
15	First North Americans	North America	Salts	Creative Kids
16	Ancient South America	South America	Plants	South American Art
17	Celts	Europe	Flowering Plants	Jewelry
18	Roman Republic	Asia	Trees	Roman Art
19	Christianity	Australia & Oceania	Simple Plants	Instruments
20	Roman Empire	You Explore	Fungi	Composing Music

2	History	Geography	Science	The Arts
1	Byzantines	Turkey	Climate & Seasons	Byzantine Art
2	Barbarians	Ireland	Forecasting	Illumination
3	Islam	Arabian Peninsula	Clouds & Precipitation	Creative Kids
4	Vikings	Norway	Special Effects	Viking Art
5	Anglo Saxons	Britain	Wild Weather	King Arthur Tales
6	Charlemagne	France	Cells & DNA	Carolingian Art
7	Normans	Nigeria	Skeletons	Canterbury Tales
8	Feudal System	Germany	Muscles, Skin, Cardio	Gothic Art
9	Crusades	Balkans	Digestive & Senses	Religious Art
10	Burgundy, Venice, Spain	Switzerland	Nerves	Oil Paints
11	Wars of the Roses	Russia	Health	Minstrels & Plays
12	Eastern Europe	Hungary	Metals	Printmaking
13	African Kingdoms	Mali	Carbon Chemistry	Textiles
14	Asian Kingdoms	Southeast Asia	Non-metals	Vivid Language
15	Mongols	Caucasus	Gases	Fun With Poetry
16	Medieval China & Japan	China	Electricity	Asian Arts
17	Pacific Peoples	Micronesia	Circuits	Arts of the Islands
18	American Peoples	Canada	Technology	Indian Legends
19	The Renaissance	Italy	Magnetism	Renaissance Art I
20	Explorers	Caribbean Sea	Motors	Renaissance Art II

3	History	Geography	Science	The Arts
1	Age of Exploration	Argentina & Chile	Classification & Insects	Fairy Tales
2	The Ottoman Empire	Egypt & Libya	Reptiles & Amphibians	Poetry
3	Mogul Empire	Pakistan & Afghanistan	Fish	Mogul Arts
4	Reformation	Angola & Zambia	Birds	Reformation Art
5	Renaissance England	Tanzania & Kenya	Mammals & Primates	Shakespeare
6	Thirty Years' War	Spain	Sound	Baroque Music
7	The Dutch	Netherlands	Light & Optics	Baroque Art I
8	France	Indonesia	Bending Light	Baroque Art II
9	The Enlightenment	Korean Peninsula	Color	Art Journaling
10	Russia & Prussia	Central Asia	History of Science	Watercolors
11	Conquistadors	Baltic States	Igneous Rocks	Creative Kids
12	Settlers	Peru & Bolivia	Sedimentary Rocks	Native American Art
13	13 Colonies	Central America	Metamorphic Rocks	Settler Sayings
14	Slave Trade	Brazil	Gems & Minerals	Colonial Art
15	The South Pacific	Australasia	Fossils	Principles of Art
16	The British in India	India	Chemical Reactions	Classical Music
17	The Boston Tea Party	Japan	Reversible Reactions	Folk Music
18	Founding Fathers	Iran	Compounds & Solutions	Rococo
19	Declaring Independence	Samoa & Tonga	Oxidation & Reduction	Creative Crafts I
20	The American Revolution	South Africa	Acids & Bases	Creative Crafts II

4	History	Geography	Science	The Arts
1	American Government	USA	Heat & Temperature	Patriotic Music
2	Expanding Nation	Pacific States	Motors & Engines	Tall Tales
3	Industrial Revolution	U.S. Landscapes	Energy	Romantic Art I
4	Revolutions	Mountain West States	Energy Sources	Romantic Art II
5	Africa	U.S. Political Maps	Energy Conversion	Impressionism I
6	The West	Southwest States	Earth Structure	Impressionism II
7	Civil War	National Parks	Plate Tectonics	Post Impressionism
8	World War I	Plains States	Earthquakes	Expressionism
9	Totalitarianism	U.S. Economics	Volcanoes	Abstract Art
10	Great Depression	Heartland States	Mountain Building	Kinds of Art
11	World War II	Symbols & Landmarks	Chemistry of Air & Water	War Art
12	Modern East Asia	The South	Food Chemistry	Modern Art
13	India's Independence	People of America	Industry	Pop Art
14	Israel	Appalachian States	Chemistry of Farming	Modern Music
15	Cold War	U.S. Territories	Chemistry of Medicine	Free Verse
16	Vietnam War	Atlantic States	Food Chains	Photography
17	Latin America	New England States	Animal Groups	Latin American Art
18	Civil Rights	Home State Study I	Instincts	Theater & Film
19	Technology	Home State Study II	Habitats	Architecture
20	Terrorism	America in Review	Conservation	Creative Kids

Unit 4-8

Printable Pack

This unit includes printables at the end. To make life easier for you we also created digital printable packs for each unit. To retrieve your printable pack for Unit 4-8, please visit

www.layers-of-learning.com/digital-printable-packs/

Put the printable pack in your shopping cart and use this coupon code:

915UNIT4-8

Your printable pack will be free.

Layers of Learning Introduction

This is part of a series of units in the Layers of Learning homeschool curriculum, including the subjects of history, geography, science, and the arts. Children from 1st through 12th can participate in the same curriculum at the same time - family school style.

The units are intended to be used in order as the basis of a complete curriculum (once you add in a systematic math, reading, and writing program). You begin with Year 1 Unit 1 no matter what ages your children are. Spend about 2 weeks on each unit. You pick and choose the activities within the unit that appeal to you and read the books from the book list that are available to you or find others on the same topic from your library. We highly recommend that you use the timeline in every history section as the backbone. Then flesh out your learning with reading and activities that highlight the topics you think are the most important.

Alternatively, you can use the units as activity ideas to supplement another curriculum in any order you wish. You can still use them with all ages of children at the same time.

When you've finished with Year One, move on to Year Two, Year Three, and Year Four. Then begin again with Year One and work your way through the years again. Now your children will be older, reading more involved books, and writing more in depth. When you have completed the sequence for the second time, you start again on it for the third and final time. If your student began with Layers of Learning in 1st grade and stayed with it all the way through she would go through the four year rotation three times, firmly cementing the information in her mind in ever increasing depth. At each level you should expect increasing amounts of outside reading and writing. High schoolers in particular should be reading extensively, and if possible, participating in discussion groups.

These icons will guide you in spotting activities and books that are appropriate for the age of child you are working with. But if you think an activity is too juvenile or too difficult for your kids, adjust accordingly. The icons are not there as rules, just guides.

☺ 1st-4th
☻ 5th-8th
☻ 9th-12th

Within each unit we share:

EXPLORATIONS, activities relating to the topic;
EXPERIMENTS, usually associated with science topics;
EXPEDITIONS, field trips;
EXPLANATIONS, teacher helps or educational philosophies.

In the sidebars we also include Additional Layers, Famous Folks, Fabulous Facts, On the Web, and other extra related topics that can take you off on tangents, exploring the world and your interests with a bit more freedom. The curriculum will always be there to pull you back on track when you're ready.

www.layers-of-learning.com/layers-of-learning-program

UNIT EIGHT
WORLD WAR I - PLAINS STATES - EARTHQUAKES - EXPRESSIONISM

If the past cannot teach the present and the father cannot teach the son, then history need not bother to go on, and the world has wasted a great deal of time.
-Russell Hoban, American children's author

LIBRARY LIST

<table>
<tr><td rowspan="1">HISTORY</td><td>

Search for: World War I, the Great War, Woodrow Wilson, Kaiser William II

☺ <u>The Donkey of Gallipoli: True Story of Courage in World War I</u> by Marc Greenwood.

☺ <u>One Boy's War</u> by Lynn Huggins-Cooper and Ian Hayward. Based on a true story.

☺ <u>Christmas in the Trenches</u> by John McCutcheon. Story of the Christmas truce.

☺ <u>At Vimey Ridge</u> by Hugh Brewster. A magnificent and hard won Canadian victory.

☺ <u>Fly Cher Ami, Fly</u> by Robert Burleigh. A battalion is cut off and surrounded by the Germans. They send a pigeon to headquarters to alert command of their position, saving them from friendly fire. The story is cleaned up for kids; you may want to point out that the pigeon was horribly injured and persevered to get the message through, a story with a real life message.

☺ ☻ <u>Archie's War</u> by Marcia Williams. Scrapbook memoir of a ten year old British boy.

☺ ☻ <u>In Flanders Fields: Story of the Poem by John McCrae</u> by Linda Granfield. Not only the story of the poem, but also a vivid background of what the war was like for the soldiers.

☻ <u>Anastasia: The Last Grand Duchess</u> by Carolyn Meyer. Royal Diaries series.

☻ <u>Biggles Learns to Fly</u> by W.E. John. 17 year old Biggles learns to fly for the RAF in France, from an author who served as a WWI pilot. Out of print, look for used copies.

☻ <u>Where Poppies Grow</u> by Linda Granfield. Uses original documents like postcards sent home by soldiers.

☻ <u>World War I</u> by Simon Adams. A DK Eyewitness book.

☻ <u>World War I</u> by Gwenyth Swain. A choose-your-own-adventure style for real history.

☻ <u>Frightful First World War</u> by Terry Deary. For tweens and young teens, but I secretly love this series just as much as my kids.

☻ ☻ <u>The War To End All Wars: World War I</u> by Russell Friedman.

☻ ☻ <u>The Singing Tree</u> by Kate Seredy. Hungarian kids must grow up quickly during WWI.

☻ <u>World War I</u> by H.P. Wilmett. From DK, this is an adult level book with lots of text and stunning visuals.

☻ <u>World War I: The Rest of the Story and How it Affects You Today</u> by Richard J. Maybury.

☻ <u>All Quiet on the Western Front</u> by Erich Remarque. Semi-biographical classic novel that tells of the war from a German soldier's point of view.
</td></tr>
</table>

GEOGRAPHY	Search for: Nebraska, Kansas, Missouri, Iowa, South Dakota, North Dakota, Minnesota 😊 C is for Cornhusker by Rajean Shepherd. 😊 S is for Sunflower by Devin Scillian. 😊 S is for Show Me: A Missouri Alphabet by Judy Young. 😊 The Missouri Reader by Judy Young. 😊 😊 Missouri by Mary Ellen Lago. 😊 😊 Missouri by Rita Ladoux. 😊 Little House on the Prairie by Laura Ingalls Wilder. Great read-aloud, set in Kansas. 😊 Worth by A. La Fay. A novel that takes place in 1800s Nebraska. Two boys, one from an orphan train, learn to overcome their different disabilities. 😊 My Face to the Wind by Jim Murphy. Part of the Dear America series about Nebraska. 😊 😊 It Happened in Kansas by Sarah Smarsh. Great basic introduction to Kansas history. Check out this "It Happened In" series for other states as well. 😊 😊 Weird Missouri by James Strait. Entertaining anecdotes and legends. 😊 😊 Out of the Dust by Karen Hesse. A novel written in lilting free verse that takes place in Dust Bowl Oklahoma.
SCIENCE	Search for: earthquakes 😊 Earthquakes by Seymour Simon. 😊 Earthquakes by Franklyn M. Branley. 😊 Volcanoes and Earthquakes by Susanna van Rose. From DK. 😊 Earthshaking Science: What We Know (And Don't Know) About Earthquake Science by Susan Hough. The latest in earthquake science in non-technical terms.
THE ARTS	Search for: Expressionism, Dada, Surrealism, Kandinsky, Munch, Dali, Franz Marc 😊 😊 Express Yourself: Activities and Adventures in Expressionism by Joyce Raimondo. 😊 😊 The Noisy Paint Box: The Colors and Sounds of Kandinsky's Abstract Art by Barb Rosenstock. 😊 😊 Dali Pop-Ups by Martin Howard. This turns famous paintings by Dali into pop-up images. 😊 😊 A Book of Surrealist Games by Alastair Brotchie. A creative book of little activities based on the humor and style of Surrealism. 😊 😊 Name That Style: All About Isms in Art by Bob Racza. Covers art periods from the 1430s to the 1970s. 😊 😊 😊 Expressionism by Norbert Wolf. The large, vivid paintings are accompanied by descriptions explaining them. A great resource for viewing a lot of Expressionist art.

HISTORY: WORLD WAR I

Fabulous Fact

In European history we jumped from the revolutionary period to World War I. Between 1850 and 1914 Europe was fighting smaller wars, mostly made up of professional armies and only slightly inconveniencing the populace, and fighting wars abroad in their colonies. The one major war in Europe was the Franco-Prussian War.

Watch this video to get the background that leads us into WWI: https://www.youtube.com/watch?v=PpJKSMoiVds

Additional Layer

Unlike WWII with its Hitler and Holocaust, WWI was not nearly so black and white. Think about why we go to war. Which reasons are good?

Fabulous Fact

Count Alfred von Schlieffen of Germany came up with a battle plan, which became known as the Schlieffen Plan. Its purpose was to avoid a war on two fronts. It failed. Watch this clip to find out why: https://www.youtube.com/watch?v=l-HeMPV5VDR4

For at least a thousand years Europe had operated under the belief that a balance of power must be maintained, but at the same time each state was trying to position itself to gain power through occupation, hegemony, or alliances over everybody else. The end result was that Europe was more or less continuously at war.

A British trench at the Battle of the Somme, 1916.

Up until WWI, called The Great War at the time, that attitude had not changed. So England was watching closely as Russia beat the Turks. In order to restore the balance of power England demanded that Russia return the newly freed Balkan states to Turkish rule. England was also watching closely as Germany, newly united from a hundred small weak states into one powerful force, built up its army and navy. England had ruled the seas for two hundred years and was the richest of the European states. Germany wanted overseas colonies and intended to take them by force. That was obvious. Germany, on the other hand, was wary of the Russians who were continually pushing south and west in search of ice-free winter ports and more land. As the arms race continued, the various states began to make alliances with one another in an effort to give themselves an edge over their opponents.

Germany allied with Austria. Britain allied with Russia and France. Russia, in turn, was allied with little Serbia, a state they had tried to free, but which was now being divided up between Austria and Turkey.

The Austrian Archduke, Ferdinand, and his wife went on a trip to Serbia to meet with leaders there. The Serbians were not happy about the whole Austrian involvement. A group with definite ties to upper levels of Serbian government bombed the motorcade but missed the Archduke's car, injuring a score of other people instead. The Archduke had his meeting and decided to return to his hotel by another, unannounced route. But his driver, unfamiliar with the city of Sarajevo, got lost. The car halted and nearby were some young men, one of whom ran up to the car with a drawn pistol and shot the Archduke and his wife at point blank range, killing them both. The young man was part of the Black Hand, that same radical group who had tried to bomb the car earlier.

The Austrians saw it as a planned assassination by the state of Serbia and declared war, rolling into Serbia almost overnight. Russia came to her little ally's aid, prompting Germany to declare war on Russia as well. But Germany, knowing that France and Britain were allied with Russia, did not want to leave an enemy at her back and so blitzed through Belgium on her way to France in the hopes of neutralizing France in a quick two week foray. Unexpectedly, the Belgians fought back, delaying the Germans long enough for the French to mobilize. The French held out for four long grueling years against the foremost military in all the world. And, of course, Britain did come to the aid of her allies, France, Belgium, and Russia.

☺ ☺ ☺ EXPLORATION: Timeline

You may want to put the dates for World War I on your main timeline and then create a "pop-out" timeline of the war, including the dates below.

- June 28, 1914 Archduke Ferdinand of Austria is assassinated in Serbia
- July 28, 1914 Austria invades Serbia, Austria defeated
- Aug 1, 1914 Germany stands with Austria, declares war on Russia
- Aug 4, 1914 Germany invades Belgium, British protest Belgium's neutrality by treaty, Germans reply, "It is nothing but a piece of paper." British declare war on Germany
- Aug 7, 1914 British Expeditionary Force arrives in France
- Aug 17-Sept 2, 1914 Battle of Tannenberg, Germany beats Russia

On the Web

Play this interactive "Choose-Your-Own-Adventure" type game involving war in the trenches. As in the real trench warfare, most decisions lead to death.

http://www.warmuseum.ca/cwm/games/overtop/index_e.shtml

It's really very good, giving a day-by-day experience of life in the trenches.

Library List

These are great WWI movies, suitable for kids, but perhaps too distressing in some cases; research before they view.

37 Days (2014)

War Horses of WWI (2012)

The Blue Max (1966)

ANZAC Girls (2014)

Finding Rin Tin Tin (2007)

Lawrence of Arabia (1962)

Sergeant York (1941)

All Quiet on the Western Front (1930)

Gallipoli (1981)

The Lighthorsemen (1988)

Aces High (1976)

The Dawn Patrol (1938)

The Spy in Black (1939)

Famous Folks

Herbert Kitchener was a decorated British officer and became the Secretary of State for War upon the outbreak of WWI. He was one of the few who predicted the war would be long, and he planned accordingly.

Here is Kitchener featured on a famous British recruitment poster.

On the Web

Trench warfare wasn't just different tactically from previous wars, the conditions the soldiers lived in were also dramatically different. Diseases and problems that had never before appeared plagued the soldiers. Read this site to learn more about giant rats, trench foot, and lice.

http://www.storiesoft-hesomme.com/the-sol-diers-life.html

- Aug 23, 1914 British heroically defeated at Battle of Mons, Belgium
- Sept 1914 Battle of Masurian Lakes, Russians pushed back
- Oct 1914 First Battle of Ypres, stops German advance in the west
- May 7, 1915 Lusitania, a civilian cruise ship, is sunk by Germany
- Jan 27, 1916 Britain institutes conscription
- Feb 21, 1916 Battle of Verdun
- May 31-June 1, 1916 Sea Battle of Jutland, Britain beats Germany
- July 1 – Nov 18, 1916 Battle of the Somme, massive casualties, no clear winner
- Jan 1917 German ambassador sends a telegram to Mexico asking them to declare war on the United States, the message is intercepted
- March 15, 1917 Tsar Nicholas abdicates
- April 6, 1917 U.S. declares war on Germany
- April 9, 1917 Canadian troops win major victory at Vimy Ridge
- June 25, 1917 American troops land in France
- July 6, 1917 Lawrence of Arabia leads successful attack on the Port of Aqaba, Jordan
- Nov 2, 1917 Balfour Declaration supports the idea of a national Jewish homeland in Palestine
- Nov 7, 1917 Bolsheviks seize power in Russia
- Dec 26, 1917 British seize Jerusalem
- Jan 8, 1918 Woodrow Wilson reveals his 14 Points
- March 23-Aug 7, 1918 Germans shell Paris
- Nov 9, 1918 German Kaiser William II abdicates, the Wiemar Republic is declared
- Nov 10, 1918 Austrian Kaiser Charles I abdicates
- Nov 11, 1918 Armistice is signed, fighting ceases at 11 am

☺ ☺ ☻ **EXPLORATION: Trenches**

At the time of World War I great advances in artillery, cannon, small arms fire, and other forms of fire power had been made, but on the other hand, horses were still being used to transport the troops, supplies, and artillery. So there was an advance of firepower, but not mobility. This gave great advantage to the defender who didn't have to move, but merely hold off the attacker. Thus both sides dug into the earth and sat still in muddy trenches, hoping to wear down the other side with attrition, battle weariness, and economic calamity.

Color the "Trench" worksheet and diagram from the end of this unit. It shows a cross section of a trench and also an aerial view of how a set of trenches would be laid out. Color the front line trench red, the communication trenches blue, the support trench in orange, the reserve trench in yellow, the machine gun nests in purple, the artillery emplacements in green, and no man's land and the space between the trenches in brown.

☺ ☺ ☺ EXPLORATION: Map

Print the World War I map from the end of this unit.

1. Color all the water blue.
2. Color each of the stars red to show a few of the major battles.
3. Draw on the front line positions in the west and in the east using red. You can reference a history encyclopedia, an online map, or the map below.
4. Color each of the allied nations in yellow: Britain, Belgium, France, Italy, Albania, Greece, Serbia, Romania, and Russia.
5. Color each of the German alliance nations in green: Germany, Austria-Hungary, Bulgaria, and the Ottoman Empire.

World War I

☺ ☺ EXPLORATION: Horses to Tanks

In the years leading up to World War I military technology had improved dramatically. Machine guns were perfected. Cannons were much larger and could shoot much further. Airplanes and automobiles had been invented. Railways and telephone lines were laid everywhere.

But in the first world war horses were still the main method of moving supplies and men into battle. The automobiles of the day were weak and unable to navigate off of well-groomed roads, nei-

---

Additional Layer

In monarchical or dictatorial countries fighting is generally left to professional soldiers. In republics or constitutional monarchies however, conscription or militias are often used to form armies.

Think about the differences and why absolute rulers would use one and governments of the people would use another. What are the pros and cons of each?

Which system does your country primarily rely on during times of war today? What does this say about your form of government?

Fabulous Facts

The most controversial weapon of WWI was gas. Gas was deployed to kill, maim, and demoralize entrenched enemies. Though weaponized gas had been outlawed by international treaty in 1899 and 1907, both sides used it. This led to gas masks.

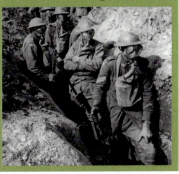

On the Web

This 8 minute video is all about the tanks of World War I: https://www.youtube.com/watch?v=zjj13U-j0_g

Famous Folks

Roland Garros, a fearless French WWI aviator, was the first person to attach a machine gun to a plane.

He did this with the help of a machinist buddy in 1915. The gun was mounted behind the propeller and within reach of Garros' arms. He protected his propeller with wedge-shaped metal plates. He was the first to shoot down an enemy plane in combat.

If you're interested in the history of combat flight you must get ahold of *Lords of the Sky* by Dan Hampton.

Famous Folks

Look up Manfred von Richthofen, aka the Red Baron, and Arthur Roy Brown, a Canadian flier, to learn their history.

ther were they much faster than a horse. Horses were of no use against the trenches since they were as easily killed as the men who rode them. Britain and France, independently of one another, developed armored vehicles to be used on the front lines. In time they added tracks to make the vehicles maneuverable across mud, ditches, and even trenches. They also added guns to make them into mobile cannon. These were the first tanks.

Research more about early tanks, how they were developed, and their importance to the war. Then create a presentation about tanks to share with a group. You should include visuals like photographs, video clips, or models. Also include quotes from people who spoke about the tanks.

☺ ☻ EXPLORATION: Sopwith Camel

The airplane had just been invented in 1903 by the Wright Brothers, but by 1914 it was already being used in battle. The most successful British plane of the war was the Sopwith Camel (introduced in 1917), a one seater biplane that was used in air to air combat and air to ground support for troops.

Watch this 8 minute video about the Sopwith Camel. https://www.youtube.com/watch?v=j6PnKUEFX8g

Then make a model using a toilet paper tube, the printable from

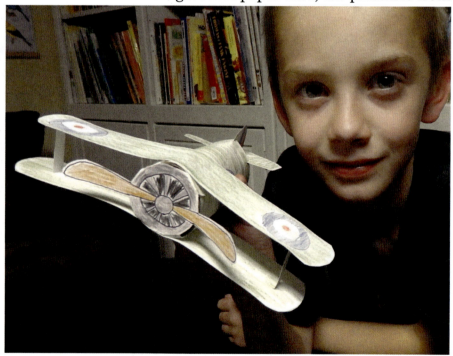

the end of this unit, scissors, glue, and colors. We recommend printing on card stock.

☺ ☻ EXPLORATION: Verdun

The Battle of Verdun lasted from February to December 1916, almost a year. The Germans had invaded northeastern France and the French rushed to defend their territory. Almost a million men were wounded or killed during the battle. The German goal was to kill enough Frenchmen that the French would lose power and resolve to continue the fight and surrender, giving Germany whatever terms they wanted. The French held out for ten brutal months against the relentless attacks of the Germans; they did not surrender; they did not quit. Down to the present day the French see the Battle of Verdun as a moral and tactical victory.

Watch this 47 minute video to learn about Verdun and its importance to the war: https://www.youtube.com/watch?v=y79-PJt-YzE

The Germans could sit still just pounding away at the French because of the German weaponry which outmatched the French by at least a power of ten. Germans had 12,000 machine guns compared to a few hundred French and British. German howitzers could fire heavier artillery three miles further than the best French guns, and they had more of them. These differences meant that the French could keep throwing men in the way, but they could not make much impact fighting back while the Germans merely had to point their guns, fire, and sit still and wait.

One of the most famous big guns was the Big Bertha, a howitzer used during Verdun. It was so big it had to be transported to the battle field in six pieces aboard trains or trucks and then assembled on site. It could throw an 1,800 pound shell more than seven miles. At the end of this unit you will

find a "Big Bertha and Verdun" worksheet to complete. Look up the information online or in encyclopedias.

☺ ☻ EXPLORATION: Battle of the Somme

The Battle of the Somme took place in northern France over a period of four and a half months in 1916. On the first day, July 1st, 57,000 British soldiers were killed or wounded, the largest disaster in British military history. More than one million men were killed or wounded on both sides in the four month battle. At the end of the battle the Germans had been pushed back just six miles, one of the largest gains of the war, which gives an idea as to

Fabulous Fact

Other large guns of the Germans also were called "Big Berthas" by the Allied troops, but only 12 actual Big Berthas were ever made.

Later in the war Germany produced enormous guns that shot 81 miles. These are called Paris guns because they were used to shell Paris from a great distance. Sometimes the Paris gun is mistakenly called a Big Bertha.

Famous Folks

The Battle of the Somme was an example of typical trench warfare.

These soldiers are going "over the top," leaving their trenches to dash across no-man's-land and to the enemy trenches. They will engage in hand-to-hand combat with their bayonets, if they make it that far.

On the Web

At this site you can read first hand accounts of World War I. http://www.eyewitnesstohistory.com/w1frm.htm

Additional Layer

In 1918, amid the raging war, another killer came to claim the lives of 50 to 100 million people from the Arctic to the Pacific Isles. It was the flu.

Usually the flu, while unpleasant, isn't fatal. This flu strain was. Instead of the usual victims of the flu, the very young and the very old, this virus struck at young healthy adults. Presidents and kings died along with peasants and workers.

The pandemic of 1918 is considered the worst in the history of the world, including the Black Death.

Learn more about it.

On the Web

We also have a project and printables for the Battle of Mons, one of the earliest battles of WWI, on our website. This activity is excellent for younger kids as well as older: http://www. layers-of-learning.com/ battle-mons-1914/

how stationary the front lines were through most of the war.

The British and French went on the offensive in the hope of pushing back and defeating the Germans in one big attack. The French had committed large numbers of troops to the effort, but before the battle even began the Germans launched an offensive at Verdun, meaning the French had to rush troops intended for the Somme south to defend their territory. This left the British as the main force of attack. The British Expeditionary Force, the well-trained regulars, had been slaughtered during the first two years of the war at ill-fated battles like Mons, which meant the troops leading the offensive were new recruits and retired soldiers called back into active duty.

The Germans, on the other hand, also short on reserve troops, had a policy of no-retreat and no surrender, which meant lots of unnecessary deaths on both sides when a position was doomed. It also meant the British had to fight for every inch of soil.

Somme turned into a battle of attrition, where the British and French were simply whittling away at German strength and resources without expecting any big gains. Later this strategy was criticized as spending blood and life for a few yards of mud. However, it was an overall success. The British emerged with an experienced fighting force, new tried technologies such as the tank and technical air support, and a real, if small, increase in territory. They also gained valuable lessons in dealing with new tactics like gas, machine guns, and hand grenades. Germany left the battle much shorter on men and supplies and much less willing to engage in any such battle in the future.

Watch this excellent video about the Battle of the Somme: https:// www.youtube.com/watch?v=XqvALkpsfR0

Make a large map of the battlefield using cardboard or poster board and paint. Depict the trenches, villages, rivers, and hills. Show important events in order by putting numbers on the map. Create a key to go with the numbers describing each event.

🙂 😊 😊 **EXPLORATION: The Eastern Front**

In the east the battle front ranged from the Baltic Sea in the north to the Black Sea in the south. Russia and Romania fought against Germany and Austria-Hungary. The overall strategy of the Russians was to force the Germans to send troops east to relieve the pressure on the French. The war didn't go very well for the Russians and Romanians. Besides many losses, the war also produced economic hardship at home. Many people, especially peasants and workers, went hungry. Germany saw that Russia was on the verge of revolt and so they sent Vladimir Lenin, an exiled Russian dissident, back home. Lenin did indeed topple the Russian government, killing the tsar and setting up his own dictatorship. At first Lenin kept fighting the war.

Getting rid of the tsar did not make the Russians start winning, and it did not give them more money or food. By 1918 Germany had beaten Russia and forced it, along with Romania, to surrender. Lenin spun his capitulation as "ending the war of imperialism."

Russia, both under the tsar and then under the Bolsheviks, produced propaganda to aid in the war effort. One of the main aims was to reduce fear of the "unstoppable German soldiers" by depicting them at the mercy of the Russians.

Draw your own propaganda poster as though you are in the Russian war office and need to bolster the confidence of your people and soldiers. What would you put on the poster?

This poster from Russia shows Germans fleeing a burning city in panic. Their U-boats are being blown out of the water.

☺ ☺ ☺ EXPLORATION: America Enters the War

The United States watched the European war with interest but felt no desire to join in. At first it was seen as a purely European power struggle rather than a battle between good and evil. It certainly didn't threaten American fortunes or territory. Also, Americans, coming from a variety of ethnic backgrounds, were very divided about which side would be supported if the country were to enter the war. Irish-Americans hated the British and German-Americans supported the Germans, but everyone else was more inclined to staying out no matter what.

Americans first became outraged when the Lusitania, a British passenger ship carrying Americans, Canadians, and Brits was torpedoed and sunk by a German U-boat in waters off of Ireland in May of 1915. British and American officials spun this as an outrageous example of German brutality. It took two more years and several more incidents, including an intercepted telegram from Germany to Mexico asking Mexico to invade the U.S., but the American people were finally persuaded to enter the war on

---

Additional Layer

Poppies grow on disturbed ground in northern France and Belgium. The torn up land left behind after the war meant that fields of blood red poppies bloomed above the graves of the war dead. The flower has since become a symbol of fallen soldiers and is used in remembrance.

Make a poppy craft to remember the soldiers of WWI: http://www.layers-of-learning.com/veterans-day-poppy-craft/

Memorization Station

In Flander's Fields
by John McCrae

In Flanders Fields the poppies blow
Between the crosses row on row,
That mark our place; and in the sky
The larks, still bravely singing, fly
Scarce heard amid the guns below.

We are the Dead. Short days ago
We lived, felt dawn, saw sunset glow,
Loved and were loved, and now we lie
In Flanders fields.

Take up our quarrel with the foe:
To you from failing hands we throw
The torch; be yours to hold it high.
If ye break faith with us who die
We shall not sleep, though poppies grow
In Flanders fields.

Additional Layer

Some people think the British leadership, Winston Churchill in particular, wanted the Lusitania to be sunk by the Germans and did everything they could to provoke such an attack. It was to be the tipping point to get America involved in the war. There is no evidence that a specific plan was made, but there is evidence that Churchill, Wilson, and others did hope such an event would occur. Churchill wrote it is "most important to attract neutral shipping to our shores, in the hope especially of embroiling the United States with Germany." Churchill and Wilson engaged in secret talks for some time, including a clandestine meeting at sea in a Maine fog.

Additional Layer

U-boats were German submarines. They were used to enforce the naval blockade against Britain and France. The U-boats, being silent stalkers of the sea, were feared and very effective.

Watch this short clip, then learn more: https://www.youtube.com/watch?v=RCrzaC4aLPg

the side of France and Britain, though officially the U.S. acted independently.

In April of 1917 the United States declared war on Germany, but its pitifully small and laughably backward military didn't look like much of a threat. By 1918 the Americans had a 2.8 million man army and loads of supplies. They also had nearly unlimited access to raw materials and manpower to keep fueling the war while Germany was running out of both. The Americans never did fight very effectively or develop modern weaponry, but the morale boost of fresh troops, fresh food, and fresh supplies for the British and French turned the war resolutely to the side of the allies. In November of 1918 the war was over.

Make a construction paper map of the Atlantic with a boat crossing from the United States to France. Glue the boat on to the map only along the bottom edge and sides so that the boat forms a pocket. Inside the pocket place the things the Americans brought with them to win the war. Include a sentence or two on the map about what effect the American involvement had on the war.

☺ ☻ EXPLORATION: Peace and Fourteen Points

Woodrow Wilson's goal since entering the war had been to position the United States to be the broker of peace and set the terms of the treaties, both to leave the U.S. in a position of power and to "make the world safe for democracy." He developed a plan called the Fourteen Points.

The Fourteen Points were aimed at preventing wars like WWI from happening again. They called for an end to secret treaties, a reduction of armaments, an adjustment of overseas colonies to bestow former German colonies on allied nations with the caveat that they would be tutored toward independence, freedom of the seas, free trade between nations, and the establishment of a world organization to enforce these provisions, among other things.

Mostly people lauded Wilson's aims as enlightened, but many thought they were too idealistic as opposed to practical. Whatever people thought privately, Wilson's Fourteen Points became the basis of the peace talks that followed the armistice. Italy, France and Great Britain signed off on most of the points, but insisted on adding war reparations that Germany must pay, severe reductions of the German military, and the reassigning of German territory.

Germany also agreed to the Fourteen Points. This was a major factor in their surrender, since the terms were so lenient. This was important partly because, though Germany was no longer able to carry the battle on, they had not been defeated in the sense that the Allies had never taken any land in Germany nor captured her capital. They had simply repelled Germany.

However, at the beginning of the Paris peace talks Wilson became very ill and could not attend, leaving the French Prime Minister, Georges Clemenceau, as the head of the allied delegation. France insisted on much harsher terms than Wilson had. Germans were enraged and bitter over the outcome of the treaty. They felt as though they had been betrayed by their own government, which by the end of the war was no longer the Kaiser, but the Weimar Republic, established on Nov 11, 1918. Later the Nazis would use this image of backstabbing elites: Jews, Bolsheviks, and Marxists, to aid in their rise to power.

The League of Nations was established and joined by Canada, France, Germany, Portugal, Spain, Great Britain, Norway, Sweden, China, India, Venezuela, and dozens more across the globe. The United States did not join. The senate refused to approve the Treaty of Versailles or join the League of Nations, and so Wilson's dream, in the end, did not include his own country.

While the Fourteen Points and the League of Nations were short lived and not very effective, they marked a radical change in international philosophy, if not in actual practice.

Make a before and after portrait of the nations of the world. In the before picture nations should be shown jealously guarding their power and seeking after more. In the after portrait nations should be shown cooperating, promoting democracy, and freeing their colonies. The portrait, like Wilson, is idealistic, not realistic.

Famous Folks

Woodrow Wilson was the President of the United States during WWI. He was famous for "keeping us out of war" and then for "making the world safe for democracy."

Fabulous Fact

When Wilson proposed the 14 Points there was a majority of Democrats in both the House and Senate. But in 1918 Wilson wrote a letter urging Americans to reelect Democrats because to elect Republicans, he said, would give aid and comfort to the Germans. This enraged the Republicans, who had supported the war, and they won both the House and Senate in the next election. After that they wouldn't support anything Wilson did. This, along with fears that a League of Nations would remove some American sovereignty, meant the idea was doomed in America.

GEOGRAPHY: PLAINS STATES

Teaching Tip

In Unit 4-1 we started a big map of the United States. If you are working on that map, add the plains states to it now. Write each state name, write in its capital, and color each state.

Additional Layer

The Black Hawk War took place in Iowa in 1832 when the Sauk tribe revolted against U.S. rule. Learn about its history. Who won? Why? Was the war justified?

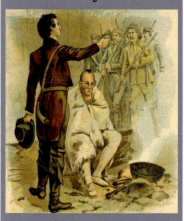

President Lincoln was elected by his company as captain during the Black Hawk War. It is said he saved a group of Sauk Indians when his own men wanted to attack them.

Fabulous Fact

Iowa is known as the Hawkeye State after the legendary Chief Black Hawk.

The Plains States include Nebraska, Kansas, South Dakota, North Dakota, Minnesota, Iowa, and Missouri. Native Americans who lived in this region include the Sauk, Dakota, Illiniwik, Meskwaki, Omaha, Mandan, Hidatsa, Arikera, Sioux, Chippewa, Kansa, Wichita, Osage, Pawnee, Cheyenne, and Quapaw. Many of these natives lived by hunting the migrating buffalo and gathering berries, roots, and seeds. The tribes lived in buffalo hide tipis, following herds from place to place.

Francisco Cornonado explored what is today Kansas between 1540 and 1542. The French were the first Europeans to explore the northern parts of this territory. They claimed the land for their king in 1682 and called it Louisiana after King Louis. In 1763, following the French and Indian War, the land was ceded to Spain and Britain, but the French regained the territory by treaty in 1800. In 1803 Thomas Jefferson bought the land for America from Napoleon who needed money to fight wars in Europe.

In the 1830s the "Five Civilized Tribes" from the American southeast were driven to Kansas and Oklahoma in the Trail of Tears. Other tribes from the Southwest, including the Apache, were also driven to this territory, making way for settlers.

By the mid-1800s Americans wanted to settle in Kansas and more northern territories, starting with the lands furthest east and spreading westward. Most of this territory is covered by vast grasslands, too dry for trees, but too wet to be desert. Because the land is flat and treeless, farmers flocked here to tear up the prairie sod and plant wheat and corn. The army set up forts to protect the settlers from Indian attacks. Eventually most of these forts became towns.

In the late 1800s the railroads arrived and boom towns rose up. Towns that were along the rail routes grew into cities. Towns far from the tracks dwindled out and died.

Bordered on one side by the great eastern forests and the Appalachians and on the other by the Rocky Mountains, and far from any oceans, the land is blisteringly hot in summer and frigidly cold in winter. Violent storms are the norm in spring and summer when thunderstorms, golf ball-sized hail, and tornadoes hit with regularity. During wintertime, blizzards can reduce visibility to near zero and trap people in their homes for days on end.

World War II transformed many of the larger cities and towns in these states into industrial centers where agriculture, food processing, and manufacturing drive the economy instead of small family farms.

☺ ☺ ☺ EXPLORATION: Map of the Plains States

Print out a map of the Plains States from the end of this unit.

1. Label the compass rose.
2. Using a student atlas, find and add these features to the map: Black Hills, Mississippi River, Missouri River, Kansas River, Arkansas River, Great Plains, and Badlands.
3. Label each state capital.
4. Plot and label some of the larger cities in these states.
5. Label each state.
6. Color the map to depict the landscape types. For example, make grasslands light green, mountains brown, rivers blue and so on.

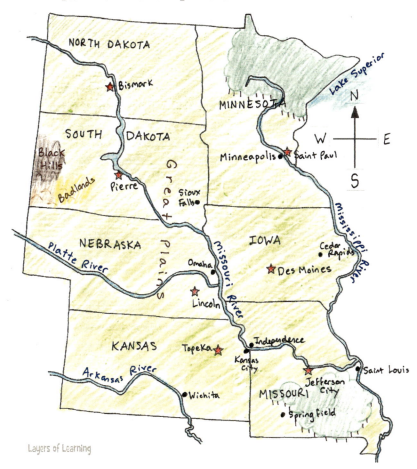

Individual maps of each state can be found at www.layers-of-learning.com/geography/.

Additional Layer

Along the western edge of the Dakotas is an area called the Badlands. It is filled with broken slabs of basalt rock, fault lines, and little vegetation. It has never been much use economically, but in the days of the wild west outlaws liked to hide out there. Find out more.

Fabulous Fact

There is an International Peace Garden on the border between Manitoba, Canada and North Dakota. In the garden is a cairn dedicated to a pledge of peace between the two countries.

TO GOD IN HIS GLORY WE TWO NATIONS DEDICATE THIS GARDEN AND PLEDGE OURSELVES THAT AS LONG AS MEN LIVE WE WILL NOT TAKE UP ARMS AGAINST ONE ANOTHER.

Did you know the United States has invaded Canada twice? Once during the Revolutionary War and once during the War of 1812. So maybe that peace cairn is needed.

Additional Layer

Learn more about one of the big businesses based in Minnesota. What do they produce? How did they get their start? Why did they become famous all over the nation? What would it take to go work for one of them?

☺ ☻ EXPLORATION: Minnesota Big Business

Though Minnesota started out as thousands of small family farms and homesteads, World War II changed the face of the state. Industry popped up everywhere and farms were consolidated into big agricultural operations. Some of the companies operating out of Minnesota today include 3M, Mayo Clinic, Green Giant, Hormel, Mars Candy, Tonka, Greyhound Bus, and Polaris. In fact, most people in Minnesota now live in cities and larger towns.

Make a cityscape of Minnesota using boxes you save from packaging. Paint the boxes in bright colors and write the names of Minnesota companies on them.

While the kids work read them a book about Minnesota.

☺ ☻ ☻ EXPLORATION: Minnesota Lakes

Minnesota officially has 11,842 lakes. In the state nickname they round it to "Land of 10,000 Lakes." But if all lakes of 2.5 acres and larger were counted it would have 21,871 lakes. 200 of those are called "Mud Lake."

Minnesota was formed of volcanism and has layers of sedimentary rock on top of that. These layers were folded and eroded. Finally, enormous glaciers covered Minnesota, dragging rocks and gravel down from the north, leveling off the hills and mountains of Minnesota and leaving deep deposits of glacial till. The glacial period is what led to the many thousands of depressions and valleys that turned into the lakes of Minnesota today.

Make a Minnesota Lakes notebook page. Start by cutting a slit across the top of a piece of card stock. Then free hand draw a glacier shape, sized to fit through the slit, on a second piece of card stock. Color in the glacier partially with light blue swirls. Draw dozens of small lakes underneath the space the glacier covers up. Color them blue. Color the rest of the larger sheet in green. Write notes and facts you learn about the Minnesota glaciers and lakes on the pages. As you pull the glacier up through the slit the lakes are revealed.

☺ ☺ ☺ EXPLORATION: North Dakota Norwegian Lefse

About 30% of the population of North Dakota is of Norwegian heritage. They came to America in the 1800s for the fertile and cheap farmland. Though very few Norwegian-Americans speak the language of the old country, they have kept many of their traditions alive and these have influenced the state as a whole.

Every fall in Minot a Norsk Høstfest is held. The purpose of the festival is to celebrate and preserve the Scandinavian heritage of the area. Included in the festival are dancing, costumes, handicrafts, food, and Vikings - of course. One of the things you might find to eat there is lefse.

Here is how to make lefse:

1. Peel 5 pounds of potatoes.
2. Boil the potatoes in water until tender.
3. Drain off the water. Add 1/4 cup butter, 2 tablespoons heavy cream, 1 tea-

Additional Layer

Hydraulic Fracturing is known popularly as fracking. It has received a lot of bad press. Take some time to research what fracking actually is. Read arguments for and against it. Decide for yourself if it's a miracle of engineering or a quick path to planetary destruction . . . or maybe something in between.

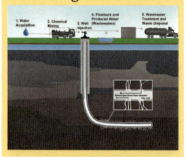

Fabulous Fact

Sioux Falls is a pretty little city situated on a big bend in the Great Sioux River. Since South Dakota has no corporate income tax, lots of financial companies are headquartered in the city like Wells Fargo, Citigroup, Capital Card Services, and others.

Additional Layer

Along with the states bordering the Great Lakes, this region is often called the Midwest. While the region has some serious industrial and financial powerhouses, it is best known as the breadbasket of America.

spoon salt, and 2 teaspoons sugar to the potatoes. Mix it with an electric mixer until smooth.

4. Let chill in the refrigerator for four hours or overnight.
5. Add 1 1/4 cups flour to the potato mixture, mixing until just stirred in.
6. Form into balls of about 2 Tablespoons each. Roll out on a well-floured counter top into a circle.
7. Fry on a hot griddle until bubbles form and the dough browns, flipping halfway.

Serve with butter and jam or powdered sugar and cinnamon.

☻ EXPLORATION: North Dakota Boom Town

Since the early 2000s North Dakota has been in an economic boom. This is entirely due to the oil reserves in the Bakken Rock Formation. Geologists have known about the potential for oil in North Dakota since the 1950s, but until recently the technology to recover this oil was lacking. Since then a method called hydraulic fracturing has been developed that allows for recovery of this oil.

This is an example of natural resources fueling the growth and economy of a state. The same process happened a hundred years ago in Texas and Oklahoma.

Learn what happened in those states when oil was discovered and then write up a prediction of what you think will happen in North Dakota over the next couple of decades. Consider the economic situation of the people, the demographics, the types of industries that will come in, the education level of the people, and the infrastructure needs.

☻ ☻ ☻ EXPLORATION: South Dakota

Mount Rushmore is the most famous landmark in South Dakota. The mountain was carved from 1927 to 1941 by Gutzon Borglum and his son, Lincoln. The mountain depicts four famous U.S. presidents: George Washington, Thomas Jefferson, Theodore Roosevelt, and Abraham Lincoln.

Find the location of Mount Rushmore on a map of South Dakota. Then make a travel poster to convince people to visit.

You may like to use this tutorial on how to draw Mount Rushmore when making your poster: http://www.drawingtutorials101.com/how-to-draw-mount-rushmore

😊 😊 😊 EXPLORATION: Buttes

Buttes are a common geographical feature in South Dakota and Nebraska. A butte is an isolated hill with steep or vertical sides and a flat top that rises out of level ground. Since buttes are so distinctive and obvious they often served as landmarks for mountain men, pioneers, and Native Americans. Courthouse and Jail Rock, Nebraska and Thumb Butte, South Dakota are famous buttes. There are dozens more. Look them up online.

This is a picture of Jail Rock, Nebraska taken in 1897. Pioneers passed by this on their way west. It helped them know how far they had come and how much farther they had to go.

Make a clay model of a particular butte from either South Dakota or Nebraska. Make placards that explain the geology of the butte and some of its history.

😊 😊 😊 EXPLORATION: South Dakota Badlands

The Badlands of southern South Dakota is a deeply eroded region of sedimentary rocks. This results in dramatic rock formations rising above or carved into flat grass plains. The rock formations include buttes, mesas, hoodoos, pinnacles, canyons, ravines, and gullies.

Bighorn sheep, prairie dogs, bison, badgers, bobcat, mule deer, coyotes, and rattlesnakes are some of the animals that live in this region. The land is arid with just enough rainfall to support grasses and wildflowers. Very few people live here and most of the land is untouched wilderness.

Find Badlands National Park on a map of South Dakota. Then watch this video about the park: www.youtube.com/watch?v=68z-B8xM8GLo

Write an illustrated report about the Badlands of South Dakota. Include a map, pictures of animals and rock formations, and facts about the history, geology, and ecology of the area.

😊 😊 EXPLORATION: Nebraska Farmland

Nebraska can be divided into two regions, the flat Great Plains in the west and the hilly Dissected Till Plains in the east. The eastern prairies receive enough rain to make them excellent farmland for crops like soybeans and corn. In the west the land is drier and the main production goes to grazing beef cattle. Much of Nebras-

Expedition

A section of Highway 20 between Harrison and Valentine, Nebraska is called the Bridges to Buttes Byway. It's a scenic section of road that showcases pioneers and cowboys of the Old West. Include it in an upcoming family vacation.

Additional Layer

The Black Hills of South Dakota are sacred to the Lakota, but the land is now owned by federal, state, and private owners, not the tribes. This has caused contention between natives and non-natives in the area.

At the heart of the controversy is the issue of land ownership.

Read this article: http://sites.coloradocollege.edu/indigenoustraditions/sacred-lands/the-black-hills-the-stories-of-the-sacred/

Who do you think should own the land? Can you see the issue from both sides? Is there a way to compromise and make everyone content?

Additional Layer

Learn more about tornadoes and why there are so many on the Great Plains.

Additional Layer

Learn more about one of the tribes of Nebraska: Omaha, Pawnee, Missouria, Ponca, and Otoe

Fabulous Fact

Kids compete in fairs through 4-H or FFA (Future Farmers of America). There are groups everywhere in the United States that anybody can join. They don't just teach farming either. There are shooting sports, baking, outdoor survival, sewing, engineering, and dozens of other categories to compete in.

ka is rural and a lot of people live on farms.

Make a barn shape out of construction paper. Include several doors to open. Cut these doors so that they create flaps. Glue the barn to another sheet of paper, leaving the flaps free. Inside the flaps write facts about Nebraska that you find online or in books.

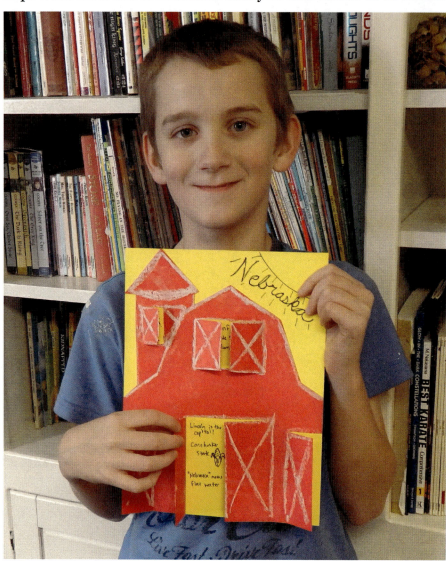

☺ ☻ ☺ EXPLORATION: Iowa State Fair

Over one million people visit the Iowa State Fair every year. The fair has been running, with interruptions for the Spanish-American War and WWII, since 1854.

State fairs were first started to celebrate and showcase the plants and animals farmers grew. Fairs still do that, but they've become so much more. At the Iowa State Fair you can watch concerts by famous singers, ride on Ferris wheels and tea cups, shop for fair merchandise, and partake of just about anything that can be dipped in a deep fat fryer. You might also see political candidates strolling the fair, drumming up votes.

One of the most unusual attractions at the Iowa State Fair is the annual "Butter Cow." Every year since 1911 a huge sculpture featuring a cow, not to mention other famous figures like Harry Potter and American Gothic, has been sculpted out of butter, butter and cows being major products of Iowa farms.

Get your own cube of butter (or margarine, but don't report the sacrilege to the Iowa farmers please) and carve it into the state of Iowa. Wear gloves and use plastic knives and spoons as carving tools. If you kept the butter clean you can still eat it later.

☺ ☻ ☻ **EXPLORATION: Deep Rolling Hills of Iowa**

Iowa is sandwiched right between the Missouri and Mississippi Rivers. Like the rest of the states in this region, Iowa is mostly grasslands, with forests in the river valleys. But unlike the other states, Iowa is not flat. It is covered with gently rolling hills, deep with fertile soils.

The soils in Iowa are made of loess (pronounced "luss"), or windblown silt. The silt was originally formed by glaciers grinding rocks to dust. When the glaciers retreated the fine particles were picked up by wind and then redeposited. Iowa is dozens of feet deep in the stuff. This type of soil is called "Tama" and is the official state soil of Iowa.

The Tama soil is very productive for crops but is easily eroded,

Additional Layer

Iowa is smack in the middle of the American heartland. Her food is all-American and nothing says America like food-on-a-stick, especially if its deep fried or frozen and coated in chocolate.

Take a look at these foods featured on the fairway at the Iowa State Fair: www.iowastatefair.org/fair-attractions/food-on-a-stick/.

State fairs invent new foods-on-a-stick every year. Invent your own food of awesomeness by reinventing your favorite sweets and slapping them on a stick.

Fabulous Fact

Many people think that farm work is all about work, but it's also brainy. Farmers are businessmen, negotiators, and scientists, many with college degrees.

Additional Layer

The states in this unit were almost exclusively agricultural until the 1940s. Two major events, back to back, were the catalyst that brought industry and infrastructure to the plains. They were the Great Depression with its Dust Bowl and World War II. Think about how major events like these can have a lasting effect on individuals and nations.

What if the Great Depression and WWII had never happened? What do you think these states would be like now?

Famous Folks

The farms of the Midwest region of the United States produce a huge proportion of the world's grains. Kansas has 20,000 wheat farmers and produces about 328 million bushels of wheat a year. About half of that wheat is exported abroad.

Additional Layer

Kansas is pretty dry. That's why there are not more trees. Kansas farmers and cities rely on aquifers for the water supply. Take a field trip to your water supply to see where it comes from.

so farmers work hard at having good conservation practices to prevent the loss of their rich topsoil. Some of the things farmers do include making sure there is a crop cover at all times and using no-till farming where they don't turn over the topsoil to prepare it for planting. The soil is why Iowa is such a rich farming state.

Create a soil profile for Iowa. Make a background with sky and grass at the top, then soil gradually fading from very dark to light brown at the bottom of the sheet. Most of the background should be the soil, with just a thin strip at the top for the sky and grass.

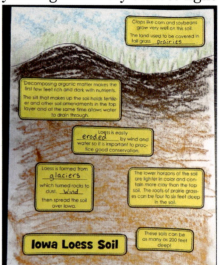

Use the printable "Iowa Loess Soil" from the end of this unit and add word bubbles to the background that describe the soil. Glue the word bubbles to the background. Read each one as you glue it. There are a few blanks to fill in. The answers are: glaciers, wind, prairies, eroded.

☺ ☺ EXPLORATION: Kansas Prairie Bird Habitats

The Great Plains of Kansas are now mostly covered with farms that produce enormous quantities of wheat, soybeans, corn, and sorghum. But there are still pockets of the original prairie ecosystem, including the Tallgrass Prairie National Preserve in the Kansas Flint Hills.

Within a tallgrass prairie there are four different habitats:

- Upland - dry, mostly grasses, some bushes, few trees
- Bottomland - near streams and rivers, flood plain, fertile soil, grasses, bushes, more trees
- Riparian - land right next to streams and rivers, well watered, trees, reeds, willows, cattails
- Aquatic -rivers, streams, lakes and ponds

At the end of this unit you will find printable bird cards to cut apart. Each of these birds lives on the prairies in one of the four habitats above. Do some research about each one. Write a few facts about each bird on the back of its card and then see if you can decide which habitat the bird belongs in. Make pockets out of paper for the bird cards to slide into. Each pocket should be labeled with a different prairie habitat. Glue the pockets onto a notebooking page. Give the page a title.

☺ ☻ EXPLORATION: What's From Kansas?

At the end of this unit you will find printable cards to cut apart. The cards include landmarks and cultural things from Kansas, as well as some things that are not in Kansas. Hold up one card at a time and have the kids guess whether the item on the card is from Kansas or not. If it is, they should make a small illustration of the item on a map of Kansas. If it's a landmark, make sure it's in the correct location in Kansas. You can get a map of Kansas here: http://www.layers-of-learning.com/kansas-state-study/.

Things not from Kansas: Grand Canyon, Statue of Liberty

(The Kansa Tribe is now located in Oklahoma where they were moved by the federal government, but they are from Kansas.)

☺ ☻ ☻ EXPLORATION: Missouri Ozarks

The northern and western parts of Missouri are plains similar to Kansas and Nebraska. But just south of the Missouri River are the Ozark Mountains, a high plateau that has been eroded and dissected, eventually forming into peaks and valleys. The region is beautiful with forests, streams, craggy rocks, caves, lakes, hidden nooks and crannies, and diverse wildlife.

Make a photo album or slide show of images from the Ozarks. Include the natural beauty as well as images of structures, people, and culture from this region. Caption each image.

Fabulous Fact

Did you ever wonder where helium for balloons comes from? Chances are, your balloon is full of Kansas helium. It's the leading U.S. producer of helium.

Famous Folks

Thomas Hart Benton was born in the Missouri Ozarks in 1889.

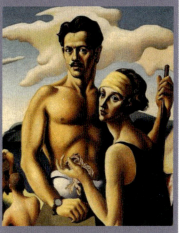

He is famous for his Midwest paintings.

On the Web

The Gateway Arch in St. Louis commemorates Westward Expansion. It is a catenary arch. Watch this explanation: https://www.youtube.com/watch?v=vqfVKsBkB1s

Image by Daniel Schwen, CC license, Wikimedia

SCIENCE: EARTHQUAKES

Additional Layer

Do you live in an earthquake zone? A hurricane zone? A tornado zone? An area with harsh winters? Prepare a family emergency plan for disasters.

Additional Layer

After a disaster passes out of the news people forget about it quickly. Do a check up on a recently devastated area.

Did relief workers help people get back on their feet? Are many people still without homes?

Additional Layer

The first people to set up earthquake detectors that we know about were the Chinese thousands of years ago. Find out more about ancient Chinese earthquake detectors.

Photo by Kowloonese, CC license, Wikimedia.

We learned in Units 1-6 and 1-7 that the earth is not one solid piece, but is instead made of complex layers. We also learned that the outer layer of the earth, called the crust, is broken into smaller chunks called plates. The plates are moving, pushing against one another, cracking, grinding, crunching, and melting. All that movement can create tremors that we feel at the surface. These are earthquakes.

Most earthquakes are centered on the edges of plates, just as volcanoes are centered in these places. It is at the edges of plates where most of the movement takes place. Shallow earthquakes happen at places where the plates meet at the surface. Deep earthquakes happen where one plate is sliding underneath another.

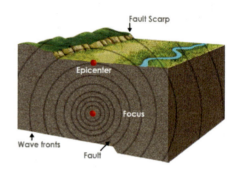

The place in the earth where the earthquake originates from is called the focus. The spot directly above the focus on the surface of the earth is called the epicenter.

☺ ☺ ☻ **EXPLORATION: Map of Earthquakes**
Here's a link to a website that shows all the major earthquakes of 5.0 and above that have occurred all over the world recently.

https://earthquake.usgs.gov/earthquakes/

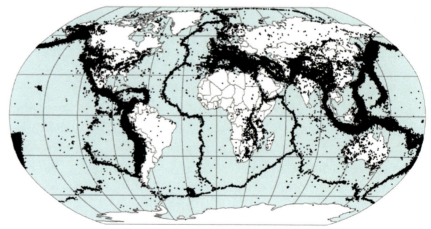

Talk about which areas get the most quakes. Notice the "ring of fire" around the Pacific. Discuss how quakes usually happen on the edges of plates where lots of stress is present in the earth. Freehand draw your own ring of fire map.

😊 🙂 EXPLORATION: Seismometer

A seismometer measures earth shaking. Basically, it works by a hanging heavy weight suspended over a moving sheet of paper with a pen attached to the weight. The pen just touches the paper and creates a straight line when the weight remains still. But if the weight begins to move due to shaking in the earth, then the pen will draw a squiggly line - the more squiggly, the more the earth is shaking.

You'll need a cardboard box, plastic or paper cup, string, pen, tape, paper, and scissors.

1. Cut the flaps off the cardboard box so one side is completely open.
2. Poke two holes adjacent to one another on one side of the box, near the opening.
3. Poke two holes into the rim of your cup. Thread the string through the cup rim and then through the holes you made in the box.
4. Fill the cup with something heavy like pebbles, coins, or nuts and bolts.
5. Tape a pen to the side of the hanging cup so it just touches the surface below.
6. Make a long strip of paper by cutting one sheet in half, hot dog style, and then taping the two pieces together end to end.
7. Place the paper under the hanging cup and slowly pull it through while someone jumps up and down and gently shakes the table.

The seismometer works in the same way a real scientific one works in a real earthquake.

😊 🙂 EXPERIMENT: Sand

Seismic waves do not move the same through all materials. When waves pass through sand they move very slowly and are distributed away from the center.

Try this experiment. Get two tubes (toilet paper tubes work well). Place a paper towel across the opening of each one and secure with a rubber band. Fill one tube with rice and one with clay or play dough. Press down on the contents of each tube with your fingers putting pressure on the paper towel. What happens?

The clay should bust through the paper towel, but the rice doesn't.

On the Web

This super short clip about earthquakes is a good introduction to the topic: https://www.youtube.com/watch?v=-zNyVPsj8zc

Famous Folks

Charles Richter was a Caltech professor and researcher who created a scale and seismograph to measure earthquakes with the help of his colleague Beno Gutenberg.

Writer's Workshop

Earthquakes are usually caused by movement of the earth's crust along faults, but they can also be caused by volcanoes, landslides, nuclear tests, or asteroid impacts.

Write about an earthquake that takes place in the middle of the Canadian Shield, far from a fault. What causes it?

Additional Layer

The 2011 Tohoku Earthquake was one of the most destructive in recorded history. But it wasn't the shaking that did the damage. The epicenter of the earthquake was out in the ocean, and the shaking of the ocean floor produced a strong tsunami wave that washed far inland with terrific force.

Many people in Japan didn't take the tsunami warnings seriously and lost their lives as a result.

After the shaking stopped and the waters receded, a nuclear reactor went into meltdown, 4.4 million people were without power for weeks. More than 15,000 died in a country prepared for quakes.

Fabulous Fact

Even though the P-waves are faster, it is S-waves and Rayleigh waves that cause the destruction. So it is possible to give advance warning of a quake, but the warning only comes a few seconds before the quake hits. Still, those few seconds are enough to stop an elevator at the nearest floor or shut off utilities just in time to prevent explosions, floods, and fires.

Like sand, rice is made up of tiny individual particles that do not simply move forward when pressed on by a force. They move sideways and even backward as well as forward.

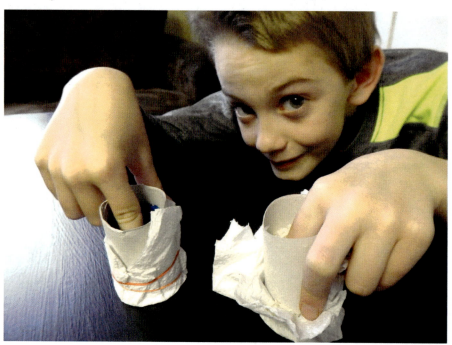

☺ ☺ ☺ EXPERIMENT: P Waves

P stands for Primary. Primary waves are the first to be detected from an earthquake. They are the fastest traveling waves. P waves are compression waves, similar to sound waves. They travel through solid rock and through the core of the earth. When a sound wave travels through air it is slower than when it travels through a solid. The same is true of P waves. When traveling through solid rock they travel at a different speed than when traveling through melted rock or metal. The change in speed also causes a change in direction.

Try this. Tape one end of a string to a table. Stretch the string taut and strum it. Listen carefully to the sound. Now take the same taut string, wrap it around your finger a couple of times and place your finger in your ear. Strum it again. The second time the sound should be much stronger. The sound is traveling through the solid string straight into your ear instead of traveling through air first, so it is faster and stronger.

Super sensitive earthquake detecting equipment is located all over the planet, and when an earthquake strikes Japan, scientists in California, New York, Australia, and Antarctica can all record the effects of the waves. It is because of the strength and direction the waves are traveling that we can get a picture of what the earth looks like inside.

Here is a diagram showing how the waves travel, change direction when they hit a new material and change speed, and how they bounce back off the surface and reappear in new places.

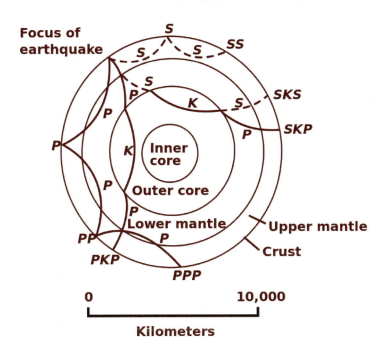

S waves are secondary waves, they move slower and are detected after the P waves. They have less energy and can only travel through solids.

The way the P-waves are deflected by the different materials of the inner earth gave scientists the clues to make pretty good guesses about what the inner earth is made of.

☺ ☻ EXPERIMENT: Strike-Slip Earthquake
Why does the earth seem to stay nice and still for long periods of time and then suddenly shake violently without warning? Why does it settle back into a quiet period afterward, as though nothing had ever happened? It's a force thing. Let's look more closely at a strike-slip fault.

On the Web
This video from Khan Academy does a great job explaining how seismic waves work and how they helped scientists figure out what is inside the earth. https://www.youtube.com/watch?v=N-hioAAdYDJM

Follow it up with this one:

https://www.youtube.com/watch?v=KLoi1RSnpfI

Famous Folks
Rayleigh waves are surface waves that move along in a manner similar to waves on the water, but are moving through solids.

They are named after Lord Rayleigh, a physicist who predicted their existence in 1885.

Besides the wave named after him, Rayleigh was brilliant at understanding sound waves.

Fabulous Fact

Besides a strike-slip fault, there are two other main types of faults. A dip-slip fault has the plates sliding past one another vertically, one is lifting while the other is falling. An oblique-slip fault is a combination of dip-slip and strike-slip faults, the plates move past each other at an angle.

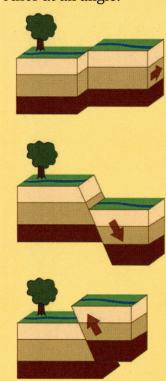

The first fault in the above set of images is a strike-slip fault. The second and third images are both dip-slip faults, with the center image being a "normal" and the third being a "thrust" fault.

Both of these processes happening at once are an oblique-slip fault.

A strike-slip fault is made up of two massive chunks of rock sliding horizontally past one another.

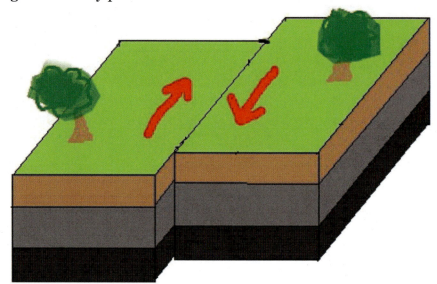

We can simulate what is happening with a brick, a rubber band, and a rough piece of plywood. Wrap a heavy duty rubber band or two around the brick. Set the brick on the piece of plywood. Slowly stretch the rubber band until the brick gives way and slides.

The brick doesn't move until the force becomes great enough to overcome inertia. This is true in the crust of the earth too. The blocks of rock will sit still with pressure building and building until suddenly . . . slip . . . you have an earthquake. Then the pressure is relieved, and it starts to build again.

😊 😊 😊 **EXPERIMENT: Shake Table**
Build a simple shake table to simulate the movement of an earthquake.

You need a plastic lid from a coffee can (or a similarly sized lid), marbles, and a wood or stiff plastic platform (plywood, a cutting board, etc.).

Just set your lid down on a stable surface and fill it with 10-20 marbles. Set your platform on top so it is more or less centered. Now you can build various structures, buildings and bridges, and test which stands up to shaking better. Shaking back and forth with small rapid movements simulates P waves. Moving up and down vertically or side to side in small rapid movements demonstrates S waves.

☺ ☺ ☺ EXPERIMENT: Elastic Rebound Theory

It takes an enormous amount of force to shift the rocks that make up the crust of the earth. The force doesn't happen all at once, but it builds over time until suddenly . . . snap . . . the plates shift and you get an earthquake. This theory, that energy is stored in the rocks as they deform and stretch and then is suddenly released all at once is called Elastic Rebound Theory.

To see how this works you'll need a watermelon and a whole bunch of large rubber bands. **Do this experiment outside. It will make an awful mess.**

First, put the watermelon in your hands and press to feel how strong the watermelon is. Then get a rubber band and stretch it in your hand to feel how much force the rubber band has when stretched. Now stretch rubber bands around the watermelon one at a time until the watermelon explodes.

Notice that the force builds up incrementally, a little at a time, but the watermelon crushes all at once, not a little at a time. Though before it crushes, it is deformed a little. This is what happens to the crust of the earth. It becomes deformed and then it breaks suddenly.

☻ ☻ EXPLORATION: Measuring Earthquakes

Scientists like to measure how intense earthquakes are by the amount of shaking an earthquake produces and how much damage it does. The first scale used was the Mercalli Scale, which has numbers from I to XII, with XII being total destruction. It measures earthquakes based on how much damage they do to manmade structures and on how much they change the face of the earth. An earthquake of a scale 12 would be total destruction. The problem with this scale is that it is subjective. One person might think an earthquake was a VII while the next guy might think it was only a VI.

In the 1930s Charles Richter developed a new way of measuring earthquakes that would be more scientific. He based his measurements on seismometers and the amplitude of the waves they measure. This type of measurement means absolute numbers can be assigned to an earthquake.

In the 1970s seismologists created a new scale. It uses the amplitude of earthquakes and connects that measurement to the actual displacement of the plates resulting from the earthquake. This new scale is called the moment magnitude scale. It is the scale you hear reported on the news, even if some people still call it the "Richter scale."

At the end of this unit you will find a chart of the Mercalli scale and magnitude scale and what they mean in terms of damage caused. Cut apart the chart so that each magnitude is its own piece. Look up images and information about an earthquake that falls into each of the magnitude ranges. Make a notebook page for each one that includes both the information you found about the specific earthquake you researched and some images of the damage caused. Note that the lower ranges of the scale cause no damage and are hardly noticed by people, so you may have very little information on those pages. Put your notebook pages in order of increasing magnitude and see whether the damage increases with the increased magnitude.

☻ ☻ EXPLORATION: Focus and Epicenter

The point at which rocks rupture or break under the surface of the earth is the focus of the earthquake. The focus can be just under the surface or miles and miles deep. The point directly above the focus, up on the surface, is called the epicenter.

Earthquakes with a shallow focus can do a significant amount of damage on the surface. These earthquakes, as far as we know, follow the elas-

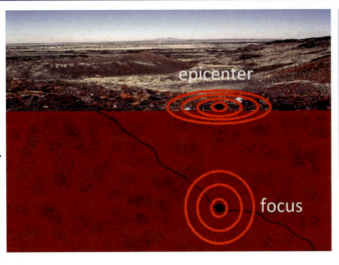

tic rebound theory (explained in the Elastic Rebound Theory Experiment from this unit). But some earthquakes happen so far beneath the surface that they were only discovered about a hundred years ago, after seismometers were invented. These are called deep focus earthquakes. They don't do much surface damage at all. They usually happen where one tectonic plate is sliding beneath another, like along the coast of Chile in South America.

Create a model using clay to show where the epicenter and focus of an earthquake are located.

Look up several news stories about earthquakes. Find the information that tells where the epicenter was located and how deep it was (the focus).

☺ EXPLORATION: Deep Focus Earthquake Hypotheses
Since deep-focus quakes are so deep, they are poorly understood. For example, rocks near the surface of the earth are cold and brittle, meaning they can crack and break, but the rock miles deep is hot and plastic. When forces are placed on them they ought to just deform, like play dough. But quite frequently it turns out they do suddenly release large amounts of energy all at once.

There are four different hypotheses out there right now about how these deep earthquakes occur.

1. Solid state phase transitions
2. Dehydration embrittlement
3. Transformational faulting
4. Shear instability

Look up information about each of these ideas. Divide a sheet of paper into four quadrants and draw a picture or write facts about each hypothesis in the quadrants.

On the Web
To help you understand the difference between the Richter and magnitude moment scales, watch this video: https://www.youtube.com/watch?v=HL3KGK5eqaw

Fabulous Fact
Sometimes the focus of an earthquake is called the hypocenter.

On the Web
Megathrust earthquakes occur at subduction zones where one plate is sliding beneath another. These are the largest earthquakes of all and can sometimes exceed 9.0 magnitude.

Look up information on a megathrust earthquake to see what kind of effect this kind of force can have on the surface and those who dwell there.

Fabulous Fact
Scientists theorize that the largest possible earthquake is about a 10 on the moment magnitude scale. There is an upper limit because of the materials the earth is made of. If it were possible for larger amounts of energy to be released all at once the whole earth would fly apart.

THE ARTS: EXPRESSIONISM

Explanation

Many of the Year 4 art units overlap. We will discuss lots of styles, but often these styles were happening simultaneously. Many artists of the 20th century could fit into a number of "styles."

You will likely notice however, that after Impressionism there was increasingly less concern with realistic scenes and colors. You will see more and more abstraction and art that is intended to create a response.

We'll look at Expressionism during this unit, as well as Dada and Surrealism, which followed Expressionism and had many of the same historical influences.

Additional Layer

During the Protestant Reformation, the French Revolution, and the Eighty Years War there was also a lot of art created based on emotion. Tragedy and upheaval creates a strong emotional response. Often throughout history the art from these times of drastic change is used for propaganda supporting one side or the other.

Expressionism was radical, completely non-traditional, and a rejection of realism. It began with painting in Germany and spread not only to over 25 countries, but also into other aspects of the arts - theater and film, music, architecture, dance, and literature. It was a modern art movement that gained momentum at the beginning of the 20th century. Expressionist art was based on emotion. Artists of the time didn't feel the need to paint a lovely scene or an accurate portrayal of a person. Instead, they wanted to paint a feeling, and they wanted their viewers to feel the same thing.

War or huge social upheaval tend to be the roots of art that is based primarily on emotions instead of reality, and it was no different with Expressionism. Industrialization was taking over Germany at the time. Cities and factories were popping up everywhere, and life was changing for Germans. European countries were building up their militaries and taking over territories for their natural resources. World War I was about to begin, and you will likely feel some of the emotions of war as you look at Expressionist paintings. There was uncertainty, fear, loss, and sadness in the world during this time, and many of the Epressionists captured those feelings.

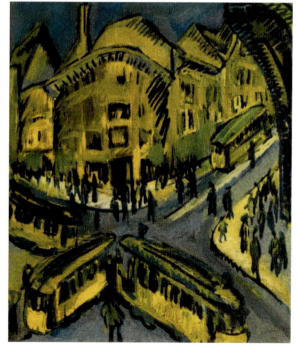

This painting by Ernst Ludwig Kirchner, one of the first Expressionists, shows a bustling city. This is actually a square in one of the districts of Berlin, Germany. Is there any peace or tranquility in the painting? Do you sense the movement and energy created by the diagonal lines and sharp angles? Can you spot the focal point that is created at the intersecting streets? There is a sense of chaos, confusion, and bustle in the painting. The yellow and blue complementary color scheme creates contrast and feels a bit jarring. It feels like the lines and shapes were drawn quickly, with the shading hatchmarks and details added hastily. The painting does not make us want to visit this place, but rather, causes us to feel that we are glad not to be there. And pre-war Berlin was not a very happy or welcoming place to be, so the painting is fitting of the time.

Trademarks of the Expressionist style include arbitrary colors, abstraction, and emotion. Look for those things as you view paintings during this unit.

☺ ☻ ☺ EXPLORATION: The Challenge of Painting Something You Can't See

One of the interesting things the Expressionist painters did was to paint things that we experience that weren't actually visible. That can be a really difficult task. For example, how do you paint an emotion like love, fear, hatred, or gentleness? How do you paint a smell? How do you paint a sound? We all experience these things even though we can't see them. The Expressionist painters wanted people to be able to feel them through their paintings.

This painting by Karl Schmidt-Rottluff is simply called *Woman With A Bag*. If you were simply trying to paint a woman with a bag, is this the image you would create? It is expressive of a feeling. The non-natural colors and brushwork distorts reality. The artist was getting ready to leave for war on the Russian front when he made this painting. It is not merely a portrait of a woman; it is a painting of misery. He painted something we can all experience, but that we can't see.

Now you try to paint something that we can experience, but not see. Make your own sound art. Begin by brainstorming a list of sounds. The possibilities are endless - sirens, whispers, dogs barking, babies crying, kids giggling, water splashing, music on the radio, hiccups, airplanes flying overhead, glass shattering, a

Additional Layer

Even after Ernst Ludwig Kirchner moved to Davos he sold his art in Germany. Art stopped selling with the economic crash of 1929 though. When the Nazis came to power, more than 600 of his paintings were confiscated from museums. Hitler put 32 of those in his exhibition of degenerate art. Kirchner was a German at heart and had loved to paint scenes of Berlin. He wrote, "We founded Die Brücke to encourage truly German art, made in Germany, and now it's supposed to be unGerman. . . I am an outsider in Switzerland, and in Germany. I have no home."

Although neutral, Switzerland had its own Nazi party. Wilhelm Gustloff was its leader. He was assassinated in Davos by a Jewish student, and it wasn't long before Hitler brought troops closer. Although still within the borders of Austria, the Nazis were now only 15 miles from his beloved Davos. He began to despair at the loss of his country and his inability to sell his art. Sadly, he shot himself in the field behind his farmhouse in 1938.

train whistle, piano keys, the cookie timer going off, a phone ringing, or a frog croaking. Choose one that you would like to paint. Think about what colors, shapes, and lines represent your sound. Decide on a color scheme and stick with it. Cut the shapes you've chosen out of construction paper and attach them to a page in your sketchbook. Add lines that represent your sound using colored pencils, markers, crayons, or oil pastels. Then use watercolor paints in your color scheme over the whole page to finish your sound picture. Title it with the name of your sound.

"The Sound of Water" by Elizabeth Loutzenhiser

☺ ☺ ☺ EXPLORATION: Munch's The Scream

Edvard Munch was a Norwegian painter. When people are asked what they feel when they look at his paintings, the typical response is anguish. He was influenced by the Impressionist painters, especially Claude Monet. He actually lived and painted before the official time of Expressionism began, but his paintings were distinctly Expressionist. He painted loneliness, terror, love, anxiety, life and death. He had experienced these things. He watched his mother and sister die of tuberculosis. He was raised by his father who had severe mental illness. His life was difficult, and those difficulties show in his paintings.

He painted one of the most famous and recognized paintings of all time, *The Scream*. This is what he wrote in his diary about the incident that inspired him to paint it: "I was walking along the road with two friends - the sun went down - I felt a gust of melancholy - suddenly the sky turned a bloody red. I stopped, leaned against the railing, tired to death - as the flaming skies hung like blood and sword over the blue-black fjord and the city - My friends went on - I stood trembling with anxiety - and I felt a vast infinite scream through nature."

Make your own version of *The Scream*. Begin by looking at Munch's version of the painting and creating your own similar background. Create the straight lines of the diagonal bridge. Use a ruler to sketch the straight lines of the rails. Paint the bridge and guardrails in many brown tones using tempera paints. Include the geometric shapes of the two men standing on the bridge. Next, create a curving horizon line and fill in the top third with orange and yellow curving lines. Finally, paint the water and land below. Pose with an anguished screaming expression for a photo. Print out the photo, cut right around your outline, and glue it on to your background.

☺ ☺ ☺ EXPLORATION: Kirchner's Colorful Paintings

Ernst Ludwig Kirchner gathered a group of artists in his German studio and founded a group called The Bridge. They were the painters who founded Expressionism. He lived a wild life until World War I changed things in Germany. He became a soldier, but wound up in a sanatorium in Davos, Switzerland after a nervous breakdown. Afterward, he stayed in the peaceful town of Davos and left his old life in Germany behind.

Kirchner, like many of the Expressionist painters, was troubled in his mind. The paintings he had made in Germany were color-

Additional Layer

Der Blaue Reiter (The Blue Rider) was a group of artists founded by Wassily Kandinsky and Franz Marc. It was named after Marc's love of horses, Kandinsky's love of riders, and a shared love of the color blue. Kandinsky called blue the color of spirituality. They created a book called "The Blue Rider Almanac" that included over 140 paintings and several articles about art.

Blue Horse I by Marc Franz

Fabulous Facts

Kandinsky had been a teacher of law before he went to art school. He kept teaching after becoming an artist. He founded an art association that included an art school. He continued to teach classes and workshops on painting and color theory throughout his career. He studied and wrote about color, line, and shape, painting all the while.

Famous Folks

Franz Marc was a German painter. Like many artists, he visited many museums and copied his favorite paintings to develop his skill and technique. He was especially impressed with the work of Vincent van Gogh.

After he was drafted into the German army during World War I, his talents were put to use in a new way. He painted tent canvases that could be thrown over artillery in order to camouflage them from the enemy. He decided that Kandisky's active, pointillist style was the most suited to painting camouflage, and called his canvases "Kandinsky's."

He was killed while fighting at Verdun during the war just before he was about to be reassigned for his own safety.

ful, but dark and pessimistic. Once he began to paint in Devos, his paintings became lighter and brighter, but still with his trademark use of many colors. Look at the town of Devos as Kirchner painted it. What hues do you see on the mountains? What colors are the streets and paths? Count how many colors you see on the roofs of the buildings. Look at the sky. Have you ever seen a sky made of pinks, yellows, lavenders, blues, and greens?

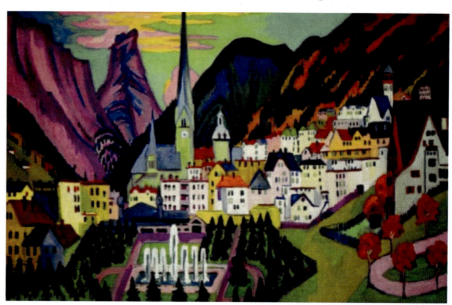

Paint your own summer scene using every color of the color wheel. Begin by making a sketch of a place you like to go to relax in the summertime. Prepare a paint tray with these colors - red, orange, yellow, blue, green, purple, black, and white. Make sure you have enough room to mix additional colors as well - lighter greens, pinks, darker yellows, and turquoise blues.

Now paint your own summer scene using as many colors as you can. Don't be afraid to make things unusually colored.

☺ ☺ ☺ EXPLORATION: Kandinsky's Abstract Painting

Wassily Kandinsky was a Russian painter who pioneered completely abstract paintings. Abstract paintings aren't pictures of objects at all. Kandinsky was a spiritual painter who wanted everyone to feel deeply poignant and personal feelings when they looked at art, much in the way that music often reaches into us. He believed color held symbolism that could create a spiritual experience for artists and viewers.

The longer Wassily Kandinsky painted, the more colorful and abstract his paintings became. The first painting is called *Odessa Port* and was painted in 1898. Ten years later, in 1908, Kandinsky painted this street in Mumau. And by 1913 his paintings were even more abstract and colorful. Later on his abstraction took another turn as he began including geometric shapes more and more in his paintings, as you can see in the fourth painting, created in 1923.

You can make your own Kandinsky art with markers in your sketchbook. Use the printable Roll-A-Kandinsky sheet. You will roll two dice over and over, drawing according to your roll, until you fill the page and feel your picture is complete. The first die will determine the color you use, and the second die will determine the shape or line you draw.

☺ EXPLORATION: Franz Marc's Blue Horse

Franz Marc loved to paint animals and believed they were more beautiful and elegant than people. He didn't use the natural coloration of the animals in his paintings, instead selecting colors based on the emotions he saw in each animal. He is especially well known for his painting of a blue horse. You can visit this website to digitally paint his blue horse painting in a color you choose: http://scrapcoloring.com/news/blue-horse-franz-marc

Writer's Workshop

Choose your favorite animal and draw it. If you could have that animal in any color, which would you choose? It doesn't have to be realistic. You could have a purple bunny rabbit or an orange and pink striped zebra. Maybe it's a yellow monkey. Write a little about your choice and what that animal and color mean to you.

Explanation

At the same time Expressionist painters were painting there were several radical groups of artists that were similarly affected by the war and the turbulent times in the world of the early 1900s. Even though they were not Expressionist, we will examine these historically overlapping art movements. - Dada and Surrealism. The Dada, Surrealism, and Dali's Dreamscapes Explorations are all focused on these parallel art movements.

Expressionists, Dada artists, and Surrealists all shared one thing in common - an examination of reality. They all wondered, "What is real?" But the styles with which they answered the question varied.

On The Web

This site, called London Dada, has more recent Dada works that include some more current Dada style protest images that you might relate to.

http://www.londondada.co.uk/wordpress/current-works/

☺ ☺ ☺ EXPLORATION: Paul Klee

Klee was both a painter and a musician. He often played his violin as a warm up to a painting session. He saw music and painting in the same light, both as a way to express thoughts and feelings.

Klee also loved children's artwork. He admired that kids could create things without instruction or having to look at examples. A lot of his paintings look childlike, with simple lines and strong, vivid colors.

He experimented with painting in a lot of interesting ways, not willing to stick to merely applying oil paint to canvas like most painters had been doing for centuries. He stamped, sprayed paint on, and painted on things like muslin, burlap, and even cardboard.

This Klee painting, called *Senecio*, shows the head of an old man and utilizes warm color blocking. Make your own version in your sketchbook while listening to violin music from the internet.

Begin by tracing a round dinner plate as your head. Use a ruler to outline a rectangular neck. Draw broad shoulders that cover the bottom edge of your page. Outline all of that using a permanent black pen.

Using Senecio as a guide, use a ruler to add three vertical and two horizontal lines across the head. Draw the two eyes to fill the width of the blocks they belong in. Continue adding blocks and coloring them to fill your head, neck, and shoulders. Choose a background color to fill your page with.

☺ ☺ EXPLORATION: Auguste Macke

Auguste Macke was an artist who dabbled in many, many styles. He seemed to be impressed by each new idea in painting that he encountered. When he met the Impressionists, he tried out that style. Upon seeing the work of Post-Impressionists, he evolved to that style. He also traveled and painted with Paul Klee and painted many Expressionist paintings. At the height of his career

World War I began, and he lost his life at the front lines while fighting in only the second month of the war.

Macke painted all sorts of things in all sorts of styles, but we're going to look at a painting he made for his family. A lot of art is made to be sold, but not this piece. *Little Walter's Toys* was a painting that stayed within the Klee family for many years because it was personal. This was a picture of special toys that belonged to young Walter Macke, the artist's 2 year old son. The innocence of these simple toys is an interesting contrast to a society that was in upheaval and anything but innocent.

At the top of your sketchbook page, write a title that says "Little _____'s Toys" and fill in your own name in the blank. Now gather a few childhood toys that are precious or the most important to you. Draw or paint them. On the back of your page write a memory or true short story about each toy you painted and its significance to you. Simple things can have more meaning to us than merely what they are.

🙂 🙂 EXPLORATION: The World At War

World War I completely devastated Expressionism. Some of the artists were killed in battle and others were just disillusioned by the harshness of war. Paintings became more somber. With the coming of World War II, things became even worse. Adolph Hitler declared much of the art of the time as degenerate. A lot of paintings were seized and destroyed. Artists went into exile. And

Additional Layer

Vincent Van Gogh did much to pave the way for Expressionism. Compare some of his paintings to some of the paintings of the Expressionists. Can you find any similarities in style, color, line, shape, or tone?

Memory of the Garden at Etten

Road with Cypress and Star

Starry Night Over the Rhone

Additional Layer

Dada artists tried to bring humor and non-sense to the world. They were protesting the war with all its brutality and wanted to free the peoples' minds from the turmoil of the times.

The movement declined with the rise of Adolph Hitler in the 1930s, not because the turmoil was over, but because Hitler launched an attack on artists and their art. He confiscated artwork and exiled artists.

There were also disputes among the founders of Dada, and they couldn't seem to keep a cohesive group of artists together.

Additional Layer

Dada art was particularly popular in these cities:

Zurich

Berlin

Cologne

Paris

Hannover

New York

Use Google Maps to locate each of these cities and find out where it is in the world.

the center of art shifted from Europe to New York internationally.

Visit the website of the Stadel Museum in Frankfurt to look at the painting called *The Synagogue* by Expressionist painter Max Beckmann: http://www.staedelmuseum.de/en/collection/synagogue-frankfurt-am-main-1919.

It is a portrayal of a real Jewish synagogue in the city of Frankfurt, Germany in 1919. The synagogue's walls are slanting and unsteady, as if they might fall. In the painting, everything looks like it might topple. This showed the uncertainty and chaos of the time just following World War I and leading up to World War II. It is particularly significant that it shows a Jewish synagogue since the lives of Jewish people in Germany during these years were particularly uncertain. The holocaust would devastate the Jewish population just a few years after this painting was made.

If you were to make a painting that showcased the state of your country or community right now, what sentiments would it show? Strength or weakness? Steadiness or change? Happiness or sadness? Uncertainty or confidence? Clarity or confusion? Pessimism or hope? Make a list of adjectives that describe what you see in society right now. Then have a discussion or write a paragraph about how art could show your viewpoint. How would you depict your scene? What kinds of line would you utilize? Would there be unity and balance in your painting? What colors would be fitting of your tone? Would you choose organic or geometric shapes to typify your society? Would you include any specific symbols to represent ideas within your scene?

☺ ☺ ☺ EXPLORATION: Dada

Dada was a style of art that followed World War I. A direct reaction to the horrors of war, it was a form of protest art. According to German artist Hans Richter, Dada was not art; it was anti-art. It was not intended to be aesthetically pleasing or appealing in any way. It was meant to offend.

Dada artists were known for taking things apart and then putting them back together in ways that felt erratic. Collage was a common medium for Dada artists. They cut up maps, wrappers, tickets, fliers, pictures, and other papers and then compiled them into one piece, often pairing things together that didn't feel like they belonged. Similarly, they created cut up poems by cutting out words from newspapers and then compiling them into random messages that didn't make sense. They also made assemblages from 3D objects that were pieced together nonsensically. The art was chaotic, representative of the chaos of a world at war. Things

in the world didn't make sense, and Dada art showed that.

Watch this "Little Art Talk" called *The Nonsensical Art of Dada* for a tour and explanation of Dada art: https://youtu.be/0B2e9CNsId4.

Then make your own assemblage by taking things you find around your house and putting them together in a unique or interesting way. Think of your assemblage as a 3D collage. You can use anything - craft items, car parts, food packaging, or even old clothing. Junkbots are a fun first assemblage to try if you've never made one before. Use whatever you can find to create your own unique junkbot.

😊 😊 😊 **EXPLORATION: Surrealism**

Dada quickly evolved into Surrealism. Surrealist artists, like Dada artists, were unhappy with the world at war and illustrated the chaos in it. They felt that rational ideas suppressed imagination, and they wanted to showcase imagination and irrationality. Their paintings often felt like the dreams you have that don't feel quite coherent. Have you ever had a dream in which you were running, but no matter how hard you tried, you couldn't seem to get anywhere? That is the feeling of many Surrealist paintings. What you feel should happen doesn't happen. What you expect surprises you. What you assume turns out not to be true.

Rene Magritte very famously painted a picture called The Treachery of Images. It was

The Treachery Of Images

Rene Magritte famously painted a pipe with the caption, "This is not a pipe." You see, it was not a pipe; it was merely a picture of a pipe. Choose an object to draw, and then fill in the matching caption to accompany it.

This is not a _duck_.

On the Web

Watch this short video about the history of Dada and what motivated its artists to crate in their avant-garde style:

https://youtu.be/dJg-zoTp82SU

On The Web

Here is a short introduction to Surrealism that shows a lot of the paintings from the movement. Be warned that there is nudity in a painting in the video.

https://youtu.be/XA_WzdlEBdI

Famous Folks

Andre Bretton was the founder of Surrealism. He not only painted art in the style, but also collected Surrealist art and organized exhibitions. Do a Google image search of "Andre Breton Paintings" to see an amazing assortment of striking visual images he created.

of a pipe that said right on the painting, "This is not a pipe." Use the printable to create your own picture about the treachery of images.

😊 😊 😊 EXPLORATION: Dali's Dreamscapes

Salvador Dali was a Surrealist painter who liked to paint dream images that looked realistic, but had an element of surprise in them, much like our own surprising dreams that seem so real.

His most famous painting is called "The Persistence of Memory," which shows clocks melting away. Time loses all meaning in the painting. It begs the question - do memories persist? Do people go on or are we all lost to time? Dali's painting is on display at the Museum of Modern Art, and you can see it on their website: https://www.moma.org/collection/works/79018?locale=en.

Since then, melting clocks that represent the impermanence of time, memories, and people have been recreated over and over in all sorts of forms, including in this real working clock shown. Can you think of anything else that a melting clock might represent? Can you think of other things that represent ideas? What does a flag represent to you? A mouse? A tree? Objects often carry meanings to us. Surrealist artists chose objects that represented something to them and then did surprising things with them. For example, if a tree represents life and nature, what does a burning tree represent? What if it is a burning Christmas tree?

Have a discussion about dreams. Here are some guiding questions:

- What do you dream about at night?
- Do your dreams ever seem real even though they don't make sense?
- Do you think your dreams ever come from something real that has happened to you or that you're thinking about?
- Have you ever awakened and felt like your dream was actually a memory?
- Are your dreams just as real as your memories?
- Are thoughts just as real as experiences?
- Can something that isn't real make you feel real emotions like fear or happiness?

- Does something really have to happen for it to be real, or is an experience in your mind just as valid?
- Do your dreams affect you?

Think of something that you have dreamed or imagined. Draw your dream in your sketchbook. Include at least one symbolic object that represents an idea.

☻ EXPLORATION: What is the Purpose of Art?

Early artists in the world often used art to communicate. They told stories through art. Soon it became a means to decorate and make things beautiful. As fine art evolved, a lot of artists focused on perfecting and refining their techniques to make their paintings seem as perfect as possible. By the time of the Impressionists, many of these purposes of art were rejected and replaced by the idea that art should capture a moment or a feeling. And not long after that, artists focused more on making us think and question. The purposes of art are wide and varied. They are different depending on who you ask. Today there are painters who paint to tell stories, to make beautiful things, to make statements, and to make us think.

What is the purpose of art for you? Do you believe it is to make the world more beautiful? Does it exist to make us think and question? Is it primarily a form of self-expression for the artist, or should it be created with an audience in mind?

Write a 5 paragraph essay about the purpose of art in your life. Include several of your favorite paintings and how they fulfill the purpose of art for you.

Famous Folks

Salvador Dali was quite an eccentric fellow. He was famous for his flamboyant mustache and his bizarre art. Besides surrealist paintings, he also made films, sculptures, costumes made of food, and even a car that he painted and put mannequins in to display at a Paris art gallery. He loved attention. He was eventually rejected by other Surrealist painters because of the way he sought fortune and fame.

Coming up next . . .

Unit 4-9

Totalitarianism
U.S. Economics
Volcanoes
Abstract Art

My ideas for this unit:

Title: _____ **Topic:** _____

_____

_____

_____

_____

_____

_____

_____

_____

_____

_____

Title: _____ **Topic:** _____

_____

_____

_____

_____

_____

_____

_____

_____

_____

_____

_____

_____

Title: _____ **Topic:** _____

_____

_____

_____

_____

_____

_____

_____

_____

_____

_____

_____

Title: _____ **Topic:** _____

_____

_____

_____

_____

_____

_____

_____

_____

_____

_____

Title: _____ **Topic:** _____

_____

_____

_____

_____

_____

_____

_____

_____

_____

_____

_____

Title: _____ **Topic:** _____

_____

_____

_____

_____

_____

_____

_____

_____

_____

_____

In the Trenches

Soldiers during World War I dug trenches in the ground. They couldn't move their weapons quickly, so instead they stayed put, digging the trenches for protection from enemy fire. The trenches were miserable though. They were dirty, often wet and cold, and frequently infested by rats and other pests. All the while, bullets buzzed overhead, constantly threatening the lives of the soldiers. After tanks began to be used more, trench warfare ended.

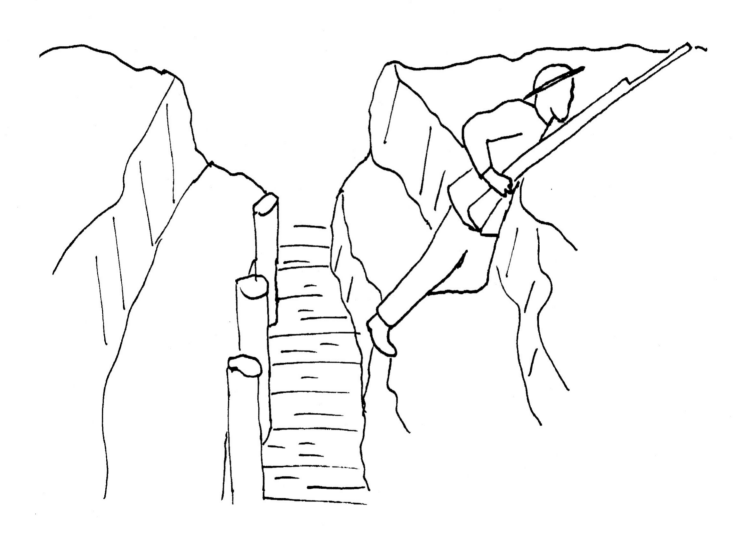

Unit 4-8 Timeline: World War I

Jun 28 4-8 1914	July 28 4-8 1914	Aug 1 4-8 1914	Aug 4 4-8 1914
Archduke Ferdinand of Austria is assassinated by a member of a Serbian organization	Austria invades Serbia, Austria defeated	Germany stands with Austria, declares war on Russia	Germany invades Belgium, British protest Belgium's neutrality by treaty, Germans reply, "It is nothing but a piece of paper." British declare war on Germany
Aug 7 4-8 1914	**Aug 17 - 4-8 Sept 2, 1914**	**Aug 23 4-8 1914**	**Sept 4-8 1914**
British Expeditionary Force arrives in France	Battle of Tannenberg, Germany beats Russia	British heroically defeated at Battle of Mons, Belgium	Battle of Masurian Lakes, Russians pushed back
Oct 1914 4-8	**May 7 4-8 1915**	**Jan 27 4-8 1916**	**Feb 21 4-8 1916**
First Battle of Ypres, stops German advance in the west	Lusitania, a civilian cruise ship, is sunk by Germany	Britain institutes conscription	Battle of Verdun

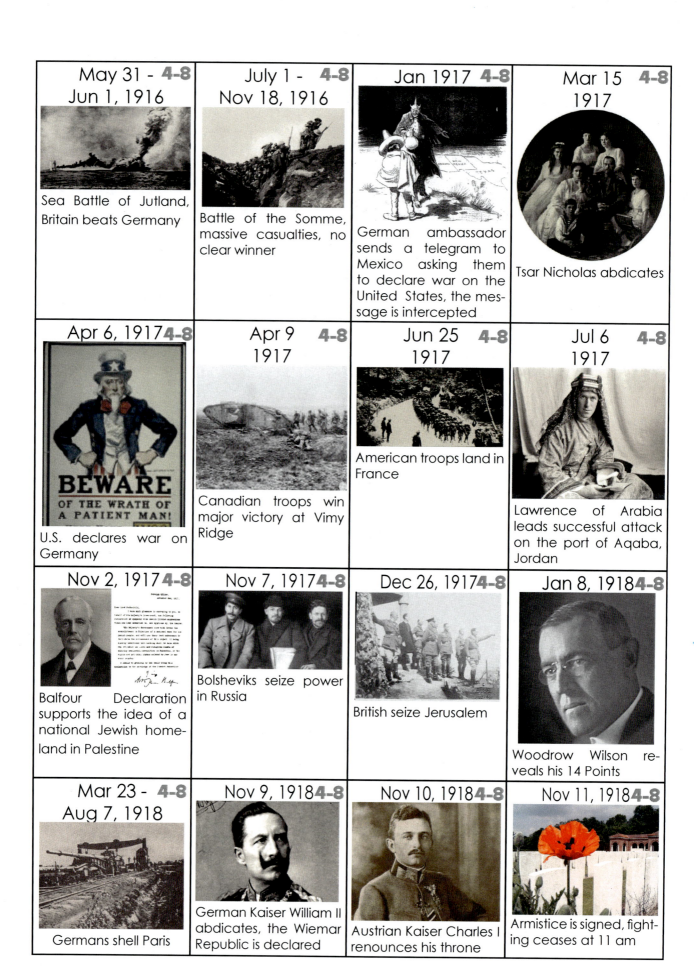

May 31 - 4-8
Jun 1, 1916

Sea Battle of Jutland, Britain beats Germany

July 1 - 4-8
Nov 18, 1916

Battle of the Somme, massive casualties, no clear winner

Jan 1917 4-8

German ambassador sends a telegram to Mexico asking them to declare war on the United States, the message is intercepted

Mar 15 4-8
1917

Tsar Nicholas abdicates

Apr 6, 1917 4-8

BEWARE
OF THE WRATH OF
A PATIENT MAN!

U.S. declares war on Germany

Apr 9 4-8
1917

Canadian troops win major victory at Vimy Ridge

Jun 25 4-8
1917

American troops land in France

Jul 6 4-8
1917

Lawrence of Arabia leads successful attack on the port of Aqaba, Jordan

Nov 2, 1917 4-8

Balfour Declaration supports the idea of a national Jewish homeland in Palestine

Nov 7, 1917 4-8

Bolsheviks seize power in Russia

Dec 26, 1917 4-8

British seize Jerusalem

Jan 8, 1918 4-8

Woodrow Wilson reveals his 14 Points

Mar 23 - 4-8
Aug 7, 1918

Germans shell Paris

Nov 9, 1918 4-8

German Kaiser William II abdicates, the Wiemar Republic is declared

Nov 10, 1918 4-8

Austrian Kaiser Charles I renounces his throne

Nov 11, 1918 4-8

Armistice is signed, fighting ceases at 11 am

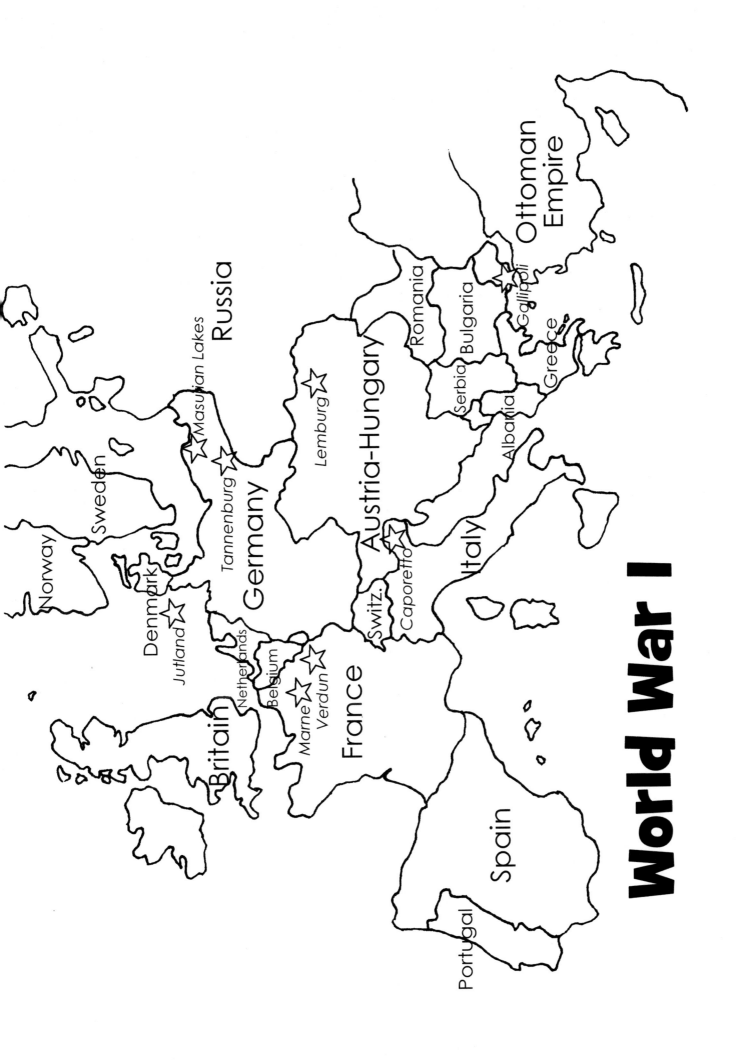

World War I

Trenches

This is a diagram created by the British during the war to show how to construct a trench.

Color the diagram.

This is a map of what a section of trenches might look like. Color the trenches dark brown and the rest of the land in light brown.

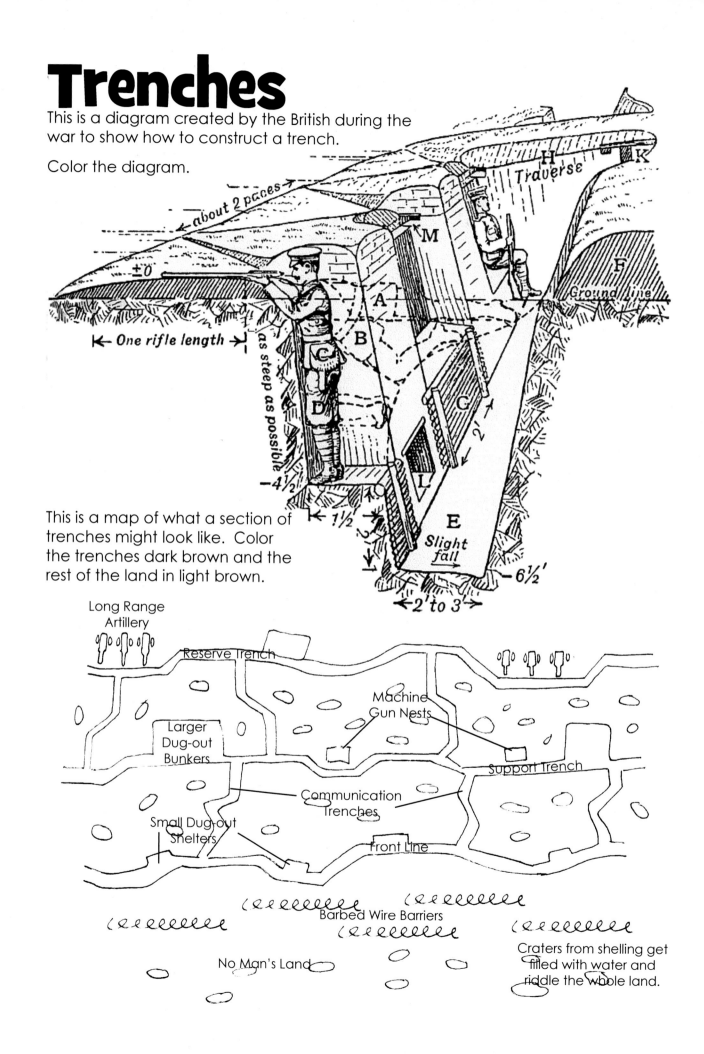

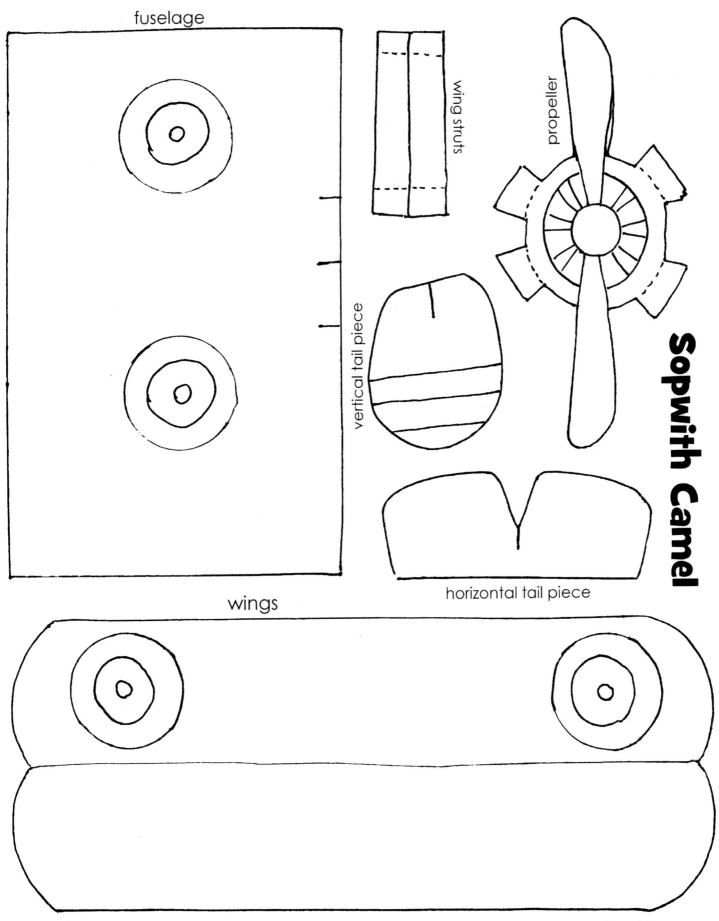

fuselage

wing struts

propeller

vertical tail piece

horizontal tail piece

Sopwith Camel

wings

Cut on solid lines (except for bullseye decoration), fold on dotted lines.

Big Bertha and Verdun

A Map of the Verdun Battlefield

Verdun Facts

Belligerents:

Result:

Casualties:

The Big Bertha gun was a massive German howitzer, outclassing anything the French could bring out.

It was guns like this that made the Germans so confident of victory.
So why didn't they win at Verdun?

Big Bertha Gun Facts

Used by:

Manufacturer:

Length:

Weight:

Shell:

Firing Range:

German Strategy

Results of the Battle

Plains States

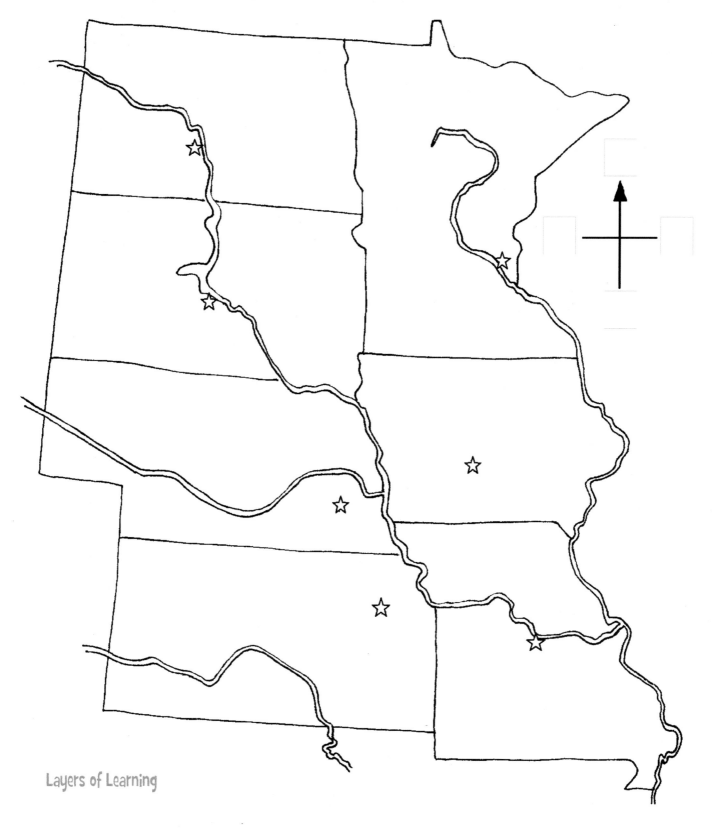

Layers of Learning

Iowa Loess Soil

Decomposing organic matter makes the first few feet rich and dark with nutrients.

The silt that makes up the soil holds fertilizer and other soil amendments in the top layer and at the same time allows water to drain through.

Crops like corn and soybeans grow very well on this soil.

The land used to be covered in tall grass _____ .

Loess is easily _____ by wind and water so it is important to practice good conservation.

Loess is formed from

_____

which turned rocks to dust. _____

then spread the soil over Iowa.

These soils can be as many as 200 feet deep!

The lower horizons of the soil are lighter in color and contain more clay than the top soil. The roots of prairie grasses can be four to six feet deep in the soil.

belted kingfisher

blue wing teal

Canada goose

eastern bluebird

eastern meadowlark

great blue heron

prairie chicken

red bellied woodpecker

red wing blackbird

scissor tailed flycatcher

wild turkey

wood ducks

What's From Kansas?

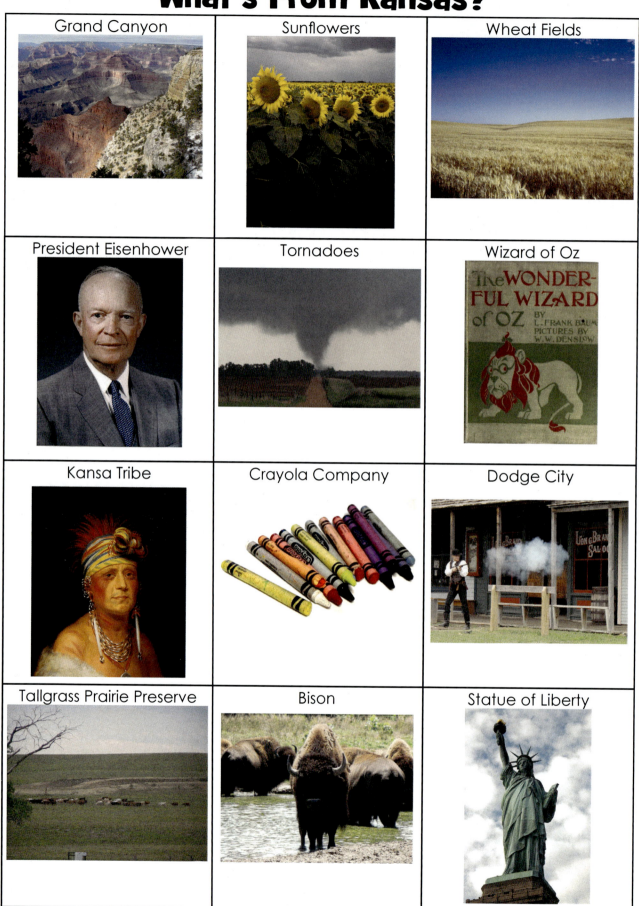

Grand Canyon	Sunflowers	Wheat Fields
President Eisenhower	Tornadoes	Wizard of Oz
Kansa Tribe	Crayola Company	Dodge City
Tallgrass Prairie Preserve	Bison	Statue of Liberty

Earthquake Scales

Cut apart sections of the chart below so that each magnitude section is its own piece. Look up images and information about an earthquake for each section. Add each to a page in your notebook with details about the information you found.

Mercalli Scale	Magni-tude	Description
I	1.0-1.9	Not felt except by a very few under especially favorable conditions.
II	2.0-2.9	Felt only by a few people at rest, especially on upper floors of buildings.
III	3.0-3.9	Felt quite noticeably by people indoors, especially on upper floors of buildings. Many people do not recognize it as an earthquake. Standing motor cars may rock slightly. Vibrations similar to the passing of a truck. Duration estimated.
IV	4.0-4.9	Felt indoors by many, outdoors by few during the day. At night, some awakened. Dishes, windows, doors disturbed; walls make a cracking sound. Sensation like a heavy truck striking a building. Standing motor cars rocked noticeably.
V		Felt by nearly everyone; many awakened. Some dishes, windows broken. Unstable objects overturned. Pendulum clocks may stop.
VI		Felt by all, many frightened. Some heavy furniture moved; a few instances of fallen plaster. Damage slight.
VII	5.0-5.9	Damage negligible in buildings of good design and construction; slight to moderate in well-built ordinary structures; considerable damage in poorly built or badly designed structures; some chimneys broken.
VIII		Damage slight in specially designed structures; considerable damage in ordinary substantial buildings with partial collapse. Damage great in poorly built structures. Fall of chimneys, factory stacks, columns, monuments, walls. Heavy furniture overturned.
IX	6.0-6.9	Damage considerable in specially designed structures; well-designed frame structures thrown out of plumb. Damage great in substantial buildings, with partial collapse. Buildings shifted off foundations.
X		Some well-built wooden structures destroyed; most masonry and frame structures destroyed with foundations. Rails bent.
XI	7.0-8.9	Few, if any, masonry structures remain standing. Bridges destroyed. Broad fissures in ground. Underground pipe lines completely out of service. Earth slumps and land slips in soft ground. Rails bent greatly.
XII	9.0-10.0	Damage total. Waves seen on ground surfaces. Lines of sight and level distorted. Objects thrown upward into the air.

Roll-A-Kandinsky

Make a Kandinsky-style masterpiece. Roll two dice. The first die will tell you what color to use. Look at the colorful outlines of each die on the chart as a guide. The second die will tell you what kind of shape or line to draw according to the chart. You can repeat the chart as many times as you'd like until you feel your masterpiece is complete.

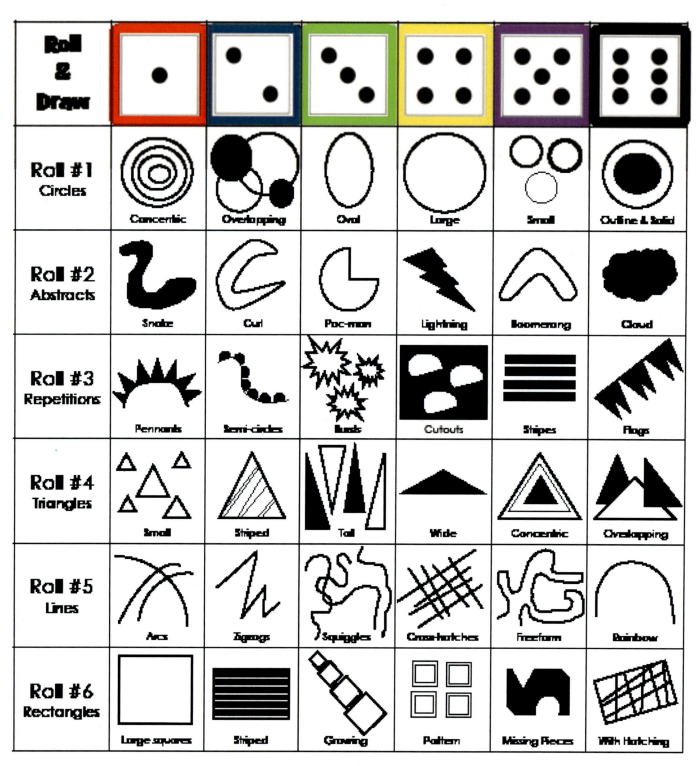

The Treachery of Images

Rene Magritte famously painted a pipe with the caption, "This is not a pipe." You see, it was not a pipe; it was merely the picture of a pipe. Choose an object to draw, and then fill in the matching caption to accompany it.

This is not a _____ .

About the Authors

Karen & Michelle . . .
Mothers, sisters, teachers, women who are passionate
about educating kids.
We are dedicated to lifelong learning.

Karen, a mother of four, who has homeschooled her kids for more than eight years with her husband, Bob, has a bachelor's degree in child development with an emphasis in education. She lives in Idaho, gardens, teaches piano, and plays an excruciating number of board games with her kids. Karen is our resident arts expert and English guru {most necessary as Michelle regularly and carelessly mangles the English language and occasionally steps over the bounds of polite society}.

Michelle and her husband, Cameron, have homeschooled their six boys for more than a decade. Michelle earned a bachelors in biology, making her the resident science expert, though she is mocked by her friends for being the Botanist with the Black Thumb of Death. She also is the go-to for history and government. She believes in staying up late, hot chocolate, and a no whining policy. We both pitch in on geography, in case you were wondering.

Visit our constantly updated blog for tons of free ideas,
free printables, and more cool stuff for sale:
www.Layers-of-Learning.com

Made in the USA
Middletown, DE
04 April 2025

73769524R00038